Humanity
and the
Zodiac

Humanity
and the
Zodiac

ALFRED F. SEWARD

COSIMOCLASSICS

NEW YORK

Humanity and the Zodiac
© 2006 Cosimo, Inc.
For information, address:

Cosimo, P.O. Box 416
Old Chelsea Station
New York, NY 10113-0416

or visit our website at:
www.cosimobooks.com

Humanity and the Zodiac was originally published by Alfred F. Seward, Publisher; Columbus, OH in 1909 .

Library of Congress Cataloging-in-Publication Data
A catalog record for this book is available from the Library of Congress

Cover design by www.kerndesign.net

ISBN: 1-59605-899-4

CONTENTS.

INTRODUCTION.

The purpose of this book is to furnish, in a con-
densed and easily comprehended form, the more important truths of Astrology, as they appear in the light
of present-day information, and to put before the great
masses of the people, in convenient form, the substance
of the knowledge contained in the many thousands of
ponderous volumes on the subject. The author, having
spent many years in lecturing, and research of this
ancient science, this volume is respectfully dedicated
to the masses — not the few — and so far as it may
serve you in private use.

COPYRIGHT NOTICE.

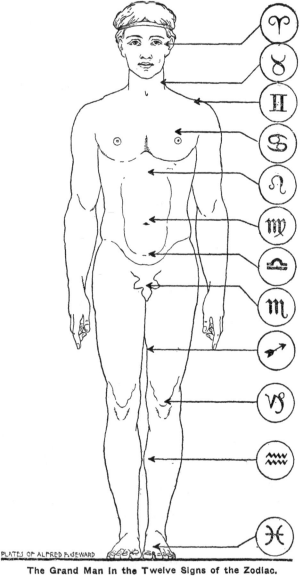

The Grand Man in the Twelve Signs of the Zodiac.
(See page 3.)

EXPLANATION OF "THE GRAND MAN."

1. Aries, rules the head, face, teeth. 2. Taurus, the throat, neck. 3. Gemini, shoulders, arms, hands. 1. Cancer, the chest. 5. Leo, heart, stomach, back. 6. Virgo, intestines, kidneys and belly. 7. Libra, navel and bladder. 8. Scorpio, kidneys, generative system. 9. Sagittarius, thighs and legs. 10. Capricorn, knees, upper part of shins. 11. Aquarius, the shin and ankle. 12. Pisces, the feet.

THE EVENTFUL OR TURNING POINT IN HUMAN LIFE.

The most remarkable or critical years in life are the 7th, 9th, 14th, 18th, 21st, 27th, 28th, 35th, 36th, 42nd, 45th, 49th, 54th, 56th and 63rd years, especially the 56th and 63rd.

These may be either financial or social crises and achievements. Health, journeys — change in occupation or professions, etc.

LIFE'S JOURNEY.

The Planet Saturn rules the first month after conception, Jupiter rules the second month, shaping and giving form to the head, arms, hands, legs and feet. Mars rules the third month, at which time takes place the formation of the bones and the strengthening of the body, and puts them in their proper places. The sun rules the fourth month, forming the organs, heart, liver, lungs, stomach and kidneys. Venus rules the fifth month, forming the face, ears, eyes and nose. Mercury rules the sixth month, forming the tongue and giving the senses. The moon rules the seventh month, giving marrow to the bones. Saturn again rules the eighth month and being a cold dry planet helps prevent premature births. Jupiter again takes up the ninth month with its moisture and yielding influences; there comes a cry and screaming little voice and another human soul is ushered into the world.

The mother between pain, joy, and anxiety takes the child with tender care in fond embrace with the love that no one but a mother can ever know. She in fancy reads the future from youth to age, toddling tot to youth and manhood, and on through life, dreaming of great possibilities and achievements that time will unroll.

PLANETARY INFLUENCES.

The moon rules from the very hour of birth up to the fifth year, teaching the child to creep, walk and run, and aids in the general development.

The planet Mercury rules from the fifth year to the twenty-third, developing the power of Brain and Speech. Venus rules the twenty-third year to the forty-first, giving the power of love and self esteem. The sun rules the forty-first year to the fifty-first, a time in the life of man when he should be in his prime. Mars rules from the fifty-first to the sixty-fourth, giving an inclination for bad habits and ill temper. The great planet Jupiter rules from the sixty-third year to the seventy-eighth, bringing the person at this age of their declining years into the true light of wisdom, a time for deep meditation, turning their thoughts to the eternal or the higher life. Then Saturn again takes up the thread of life at the seventy-eighth milestone along life's way and remains until the end of human existence on this earth.

7

THE GREAT DIAL — THE ZODIAC

Around which all the planets revolve, giving their names in their respective order as they pass through space on their perpetual journey of millions of miles through the heavens: Aries, Taurus, Gemini, Cancer, Leo, Virgo, Libra, Scorpio, Sagittarius, Capricorn, Aquarius, and Pisces.

The sun is the center of our solar system around which all these planets revolve.

In appearance however, one would get the impression that the sun revolved through the Zodiac once in 365 days and remaining in each of the 12 signs about 30 days. This is an illusion of the mind, for in reality it is the earth that revolves around the sun. Wishing to make this clear to the average mind, I will enumerate them, giving the velocity at which they travel.

The first planet from the Sun is Mercury, which completes its revolution through the Zodiac in 87 days and 23 hours, traveling at the rate of 110,000 miles an hour.

Venus, the second planet from the sun, completes her revolution around the Zodiac in 224 days and 7 hours, traveling at the rate of 12,000 miles an hour.

The Earth is next in order, and we pass through the Zodiac once every year, consisting of 365 days, traveling through space at the rate of 68,856 miles an hour.

The satellite of our Earth, the Moon, passes through the Zodiac from one New Moon to another, in 29 days, 12 hours, 44 minutes, and 3 seconds, traveling at the rate of 2,290 miles an hour.

The next planet in order is Mars, appearing to pass through the Zodiac once every 686 days, 22 hours, 18 minutes, traveling at the rate of 54,000 miles an hour.

Jupiter is the next planet and revolves through the

8

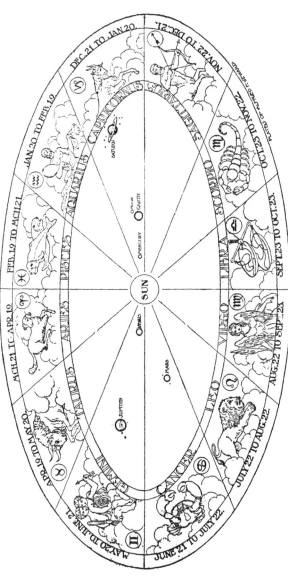

Strife and disorder is most certain to arise sooner or later when those born in opposite signs become associated, for instance Cancer and Capricornus, Leo and Acquarius, etc., are not in harmony and while for a time there may be a fancied attraction for each other, they surely will disagree and quarrel in the end. Their temperaments are such that they never seem to understand each other's motives.

Zodiac once every 11 years, 314 days, and 12 hours, traveling at the rate of 30,000 miles an hour.

Saturn revolves around the Zodiac once in 29 years, 167 days, and 5 hours, traveling at the rate of 20,800 miles an hour.

Uranus revolves around the Zodiac every 83 years, 150 days, and 18 hours.

Neptune revolves around the Zodiac every 164 years.

The illusion referred to might be illustrated in the following way: if we were seated in a railway coach at a station and on looking out of the window as the train started slowly on its way it would be difficult to determine the direction in which you were moving.

To any person who has never seen the dial of a clock, it would be quite a difficult problem to explain how one could tell the exact time of day by it, equally so in casting a horoscope to those who are not familiar with the inner workings of such. Astronomy, the dial of a clock, and the casting of a horoscope are all in reality, but scientific mathematics after all.

PREFACE.

"If, as we know, the planets have an influence upon
the earth's magnetic and physical currents, then the
conclusion is irresistible that they must have an influence upon mankind, for man is but an atom or par-
ticle of a harmonious whole. He partakes of every
element of the universe, and is, therefore, subject to
the grand laws of eternal and immutable harmony."—
Erickson.

*   *   *   *

Every human being on this earth is by right of
birth endowed with some genius or talent. This genius
or talent depends upon the rhythmic harmonies of the
majestic universal orchestra of nature, playing upon
the physical human organism.

Not to realize one's genius or talent is to be buffeted
and tossed aimlessly about by the storms and billows
of existence; while to be in a condition at all times to
recognize and receive opportunities is to live in the
native sphere from whence all harmonies proceed.

To the intelligent mind there is no such thing as
fatality or luck. Such puerile beliefs are the refuge
of weak and ignorant souls.

The spiritual man is absolute master over every
physical condition, because mind inevitably and eter-
nally triumphs over matter.

The recondite laws affect only the physical body,
and are ever amendable to the intelligent action of the
mind and will.

The body is what the mind makes it, and, of itself,
is of no more account than a lump of clay or a clod
of earth — which, indeed, what the human body is.

Man's corporeal nature, or animal soul, is formed
in the life of the physical body, hence man derives
his natural, animal soul from the life of the objective
natural man and of the human body, generated by man
himself, just as the natural instincts of the beasts of

11

the field are generated by the physical bodies of their parents.

The spiritual soul, or the Divine Human, is the immortal individuality which is formed by the Divine breath — spirit, or Holy Ghost. The essential soul-action is from God, the life principle of the universe, manifested locally and physically in animated humanity.

Every human being has, somewhere along life's journey, a spiritual mission, and it is for the accomplishment of this mission that God has created each individual and endowed each one with the genius or talent necessary for the work.

Those who recognize their higher calling and develop their capabilities, so as to fulfill their purposes, — to them alone is given the most supreme power and strength and glory.

From the growth and illumination of the spiritual or immortal soul springs individuality and true blessedness.

From the reason, mind and will of the physical and corporeal man, and from the desires, appetites, passions and phantasies of natural, animal man, arise all the strife and discord of human existence.

Ignorance wilfully shuts its eyes and proclaims itself to be right, while it is in fact the principal source of human misery.

To the thoughtful and intelligent person who aspires to go onward and upward, the way is clearly and plainly indicated by the truths of Astrology.

This modest work on this mighty theme has been prepared for the benefit of the masses, and its sole aim is to carry hope and confidence into the hearts of all who read it, and to inspire them to do more and better things.

The true philosophy of living is here set forth. Those who will read this book and follow its teachings carefully and persistently can succeed in all proper ambitions and become happy, peaceful, prosperous and helpful.

The truths printed here are the result of deep study,

careful research and profound thought on the science of Astrology.

This science is pure mathematics, and there is no random guess-work about it. From the positions of the planets, as determined by the observatories, it calculates the difference of time and place to ascertain the correct latitude and longitude of the birth-place of any given person, and from this data, "casts the horoscope."

Given the hour and place of birth of any individual anywhere, a capable astrologer will, without hesitation or uncertainty, accurately delineate the nature and characteristics of the subject, and indicate the important events of his or her life. And if the same data be presented to astrologers as widely separated as the confines of earth will permit, the results will be exactly alike from each, differing only in language or form of speech.

So, too, any astrologer will take a horoscope already cast, and knowing nothing but the sex of the subject, guided by the relative positions of the symbols employed, will read therefrom, as from an open book in his mother tongue, the nature, abilities, tendencies, intellectual qualifications and principal events of the life of the individual whose horoscope he beholds.

The art and practice of Astrology is purely judicial, and this element of its usefulness has descended from a period so remote as to antedate not only history but even tradition.

The twelve signs of the Zodiac represent the physical framework of the human being; or, in other words, the human being is but a vessel of heat, motion and vibration, swept by and responding to magnetic and planetary currents, solar fluids, active thought currents, and waves of light and sound, the influence and sway of which vary in power and effect in accordance with the position of the sun and other planets at the time of the birth.

Astrology points out and explains the effect of certain planetary conditions, and in no uncertain manner,

teaches us what we should do to control and **direct our**
natural tendencies in order that we may **advance to-**
ward complete health, happiness and contentment.

Immortal souls inhabit the bodies of all human beings, no matter what their station in life — no matter
how high or how low they may be, spiritually, mentally
or morally. This soul comes from the Great Universal
Soul, or God, and is a part of it, — a part of the
Great One.

This soul is eternal. It cannot be lost or destroyed,
and when mankind realizes this truth, their doubts and
fears vanish forever and give place to joy and hope
and eternal peace.

God intended us to be physically strong and vigorous, and, to fulfill His will, we must let our hearts
be filled with love and not fear. We must live aright,
purifying our minds and our bodies.

These are the plain teachings of science and of religion. Astrology comes to our aid by showing us
unmistakably our weaknesses and evil tendencies, and
instructs us how to attain a state in which we can
command and control opposing forces and become
giants of strength and power. These hidden forces of
the universe are more numerous and powerful than
those we recognize by our physical senses.

Astrology also teaches us to know and utilize these
forces. As a science and an art it is true. It does
what it promises. It submits to any conceivable test.
It is not contrary to freedom of will, nor to religious
belief, nor to exact science. As a study it is most
absorbing and fascinating, and as an art it is one of
the most valuable and beneficial to humanity.

It is a historical truth that the strength and beauty
of the children of the Greeks and Ancient Egyptians
were due to the great repute enjoyed by Astrology
among these people, who were governed in their marriages and in the rearing of their children by the advice of the eminent practitioners of this Art in that
period.

In all ages the wise have given due weight to the

teachings of this science, while the ignorant and foolish have regarded it as a sort of "fortune telling" scheme.

Of recent years, however, the advance of Astrology has been extraordinary. It is becoming more and more popular among the educated and intellectual classes, who are fast coming to realize its vast potentiality for the good of mankind.

Astrology is learned from books dating back to translations from the Chaldean and Arabic into Greek and Latin and from these tongues into modern languages. There are in the world today more than thirty-five thousand complete volumes in many languages on this most fascinating and instructive study of super-human influences on human life.

Most of these works are too voluminous and too deeply erudite to be readily comprehended and applied by the vast majority of people, and this fact is the reason for the present work, with its simplicity of language and its easily mastered lessons.

The scope of this work forbids the giving of details, but we have arranged herein delineations of character which will apply to persons born under each of the signs of the Zodiac, and the work contains an epitome of all that the most eminent and distinguished Astrologer could convey.

Astrology is based upon the study and comparison of hundreds of thousands of individual horoscopes, and with the march of time and more complete understanding of the subject many new confirmations of its basic truths are developed, as well as broader and truer light on points that may have been somewhat obscured in the past.

The experience of the world with electricity affords a parallel to this science. Today we readily accept and utilize various manifestations of electrical energy, that a generation ago would have seemed impossible, supernatural and contrary to every teaching of our minds. Yet to those who studied the elusive force, these things had been dimly foreshadowed for years, and only awaited the fuller development of human understanding to become actual, useful realities, familiar to all.

So with Astrology. Its mighty truths, based on the unchanging harmony of the inconceivable majesty of the universe, were not fully revealed to its ancient devotees, but have been worked out and demonstrated and made plain by the countless ages of study and contemplation and practice.

As a matter of fact, people in all ages, although ignorant of the existence of the science of Astrology, have been influenced and guided in many of the homely affairs of life by the position of the planets, and our own great-grand parents placed the utmost confidence in the wisdom of such a course.

"The Grand Man" in the familiar almanac illustration of the signs of the Zodiac, was, by astronomers and astrologers, placed in the center of the circle, surrounded by the twelve signs. Beginning with the sign Aries at the head and proceeding on down to Pisces, at the feet, each sign points to the weak or vulnerable parts of the body of the "Grand Man."

Aries, it will be observed, directs attention to the head, Taurus to the neck, Gemini to the arms, and so on to each member of the anatomy.

Those signs nearest the head of any triplicity always illuminate and assist in developing the spiritual and intellectual faculties, while those below them give power to all the functions of mind and body.

There is a natural attraction existing between persons born in opposite signs of the Zodiac. For illustration, Aries is the head sign and is opposite Libra; Taurus is exactly opposite Scorpio, and so on around the entire circle.

The greatest success in the world, and harmony and congeniality in the marriage relation, result when this attraction of opposites is observed, and this is especially true when the opposing signs are polarized together by the moon.

The children springing from such unions, if the parents are moral and upright, are strong and healthy.

Another principle of attraction is very marked, and that is the attraction existing between one born in any given sign and one born in an adjoining sign. Thus there would be a natural sympathy between those born in Taurus and those born in Aries or Gemini. Of course, exceptions to this principle occur where exceedingly adverse conditions exist in one or the other of the parties through habits of life.

In marriage or business relations between persons in adjoining signs, those in the sign below are inclined, and usually find it profitable, to look up to and counsel with those in the higher sign.

The twelve signs of the Zodiac are divided in four trinities or triplicities, — the "Fire Triplicity," "Air Triplicity," "Earth Triplicity" and "Water Triplicity."

In the Fire Triplicity are — ARIES, LEO, and SAGITTARIUS.

In the Air Triplicity — GEMINI, LIBRA, and AQUARIUS.

In the Earth Triplicity — TAURUS, VIRGO, and CAPRICORN.

In the Water Triplicity — CANCER, SCORPIO, and PISCES.

Frequently a person born in the last sign of a trinity is strongly attracted by one of the opposite sex in the first sign of another trinity, and receives from that one consolation and help in distress. Sometimes this natural attraction is mistaken for love, especially by those born in Sagittarius. This is a serious error for those of this sign, because of their strong tenacity to an ideal love.

With these prefatory remarks we introduce our readers to our work, which has been inspired by a sincere desire to spread the knowledge of this highly beneficial science as widely as may be in our power.

We commend the study of this work to all who are inspired with ambition to make the most of their lives

2

and their opportunities. We know that Astrology infallibly points to the true path to power and peace and comfort, and that to each human soul is given the right and the power to achieve for itself the utmost happiness and to bless its fellows with the utmost helpfulness, through understanding and application of the teachings of this science.

With kindest wishes, the author

ALFRED F. SEWARD,
Author and Publisher,
1566 Bryden Road,
Columbus, Ohio.

SPECIAL HOROSCOPES.

The Author, in the course of his many lectures, has often been requested (and especially since the first edition of this book came from the press), for a more lengthy detailed delineation of the characteristics of those born in the different signs of the Zodiac. I have recently arranged a system whereby I will issue a "Geocentric Horoscope" the first of each year that will enable you to know the future and prepare for coming events in advance.

An astronomer foretells years in advance the exact time of an eclipse of the sun or the moon, the transit of the comets through the heavens as well as giving weather reports and other valuable information.

As a qualified astrologer I cast horoscopes that deal with human life, fully covering the more important matters in your life during the year, with a prospectus for the following one showing business opportunities, investments, love, marriage, accidents, and all important matters by giving either your birthday or the zodiacal sign in which you were born.

A horoscope of this character will be of immense value to any one, indicating infallibly the natural tendencies of character, the faults and ailments most necessary to be guarded against, the occupation or profession in which the greatest success is likely to be possible, and the talents which can be cultivated with greatest profit to the individual.

The teachings of Astrology are so clear, its value so well established and so often proved, that it should be consulted on every important matter in life. Those who contemplate engaging in business, choosing a profession, undertaking new enterprises, or assuming responsibilities of any character, will learn from an astrological horoscope whether the proposed step is one within the range of their powers, and whether it holds promise of success.

Such a knowledge is priceless to young folks starting out in life.

How many parents of today squander their time and money in fitting and educating their children for a calling in life that they are not adapted to and can never fulfill?

How many lives of promising young men have been wrecked by this one cause alone? It is then that they recklessly squander the wealth that was so laboriously acquired by their parents as soon as they come into possession of it, and in so doing they almost invariably fall to the very bottom rung of the ladder, and after a life of dissipation and dishonor with failure in the attempt to rise again, it's then that life's young dream is over; with lost confidence, lack of energy and self-respect, they awake to find themselves on a bench in a park pennyless and friendless.

It is this class of men, exactly, young men who had every possibility in life for advancement and if they but knew the path that would lead to success and great achievements.

This class has come under the personal observation of the author of this work. In our great cities, New York and Chicago, some of the most hopeless and wretched sights I have ever beheld were in Mulberry Bend and City Hall Park, New York, and on making close inquiry I found that a great percent. of these unfortunates were born of good parents, many of them being well to do, their faces even yet showing traces of culture and refinement. This can easily be verified by the Bread-Line on lower Broadway — the Sunday morning breakfast association and the chain of Mills houses, an excellent illustration of the existing conditions.

To parents, such charts of their children's character will provide a reliable guide to the wisest method of rearing their offspring; and will enable them to give to each child the training and treatment it must have to develop its highest possibilities.

The charge for each chart or horoscope is $3.50,

which should be sent (postoffice order or bank draft, payable to the author) with the necessary information. Address the author and publisher,

ALFRED F. SEWARD,
Author and Publisher,
1566 Bryden Road,
Columbus, Ohio.

NOTICE.

For the convenience of those wishing to order one of my special horoscopes, I wish to state that after many years of experience that I have had little if any mail to go astray, when properly addressed, therefore if more convenient you may enclose (a dollar bill) with the above coupon which will be found perfectly safe.

THE AUTHOR.

CAUTION. Never enter upon a business career, or make any important changes without a Horoscope, it might be the means of retaining the savings of a lifetime — also covers Love and Marriage, as well as all important matters in your life.

Order today. Sealed in plain envelope.

ARIES.

(March 21 to April 19.)

Those who are born under this sign should appreciate the fact that theirs is the most favorable birth-sign in the Zodiac.

Aries people usually possess extraordinary characters, and are remarkable for their enterprise, brilliancy and high executive ability. If they will assimilate the great truths taught by the science of Astrology, resolve to possess themselves of their heaven-sent heritage, and resolutely turn from the weaknesses and faults that threaten them, they can win success beyond measure; honor, esteem, position, power, health and love will be theirs without limit.

Aries nature is frequently distinguished by its great retentiveness, being able to memorize hundreds of details and recall them at will, as well as possessing great insight into the responsibility of humanity. They deal in the truth and are quick to see the folly in the prevarications of others. When once the confidence of the Aries person is lost, it is seldom if ever regained, though they seldom hold a grudge against even their bitterest enemies — simply, you go your way and I mine.

The taller Aries people seem to have the spiritual phase of their natures more strongly marked. Their generosity is very great, they are continually seeking to do good to others, and they do not amass wealth as easily as do their shorter brothers. Striking occult powers can be developed by such persons if they give their minds to deep study.

There are two types of Aries people, the former one being that of a strong well proportioned body of powerful frame. The shoulders being quite broad, though at times an inclination to slenderness. This type usually has a high, broad well rounded forehead. The eyes are well set and have an intellectual twinkle with much hypnotic force.

The complexion is usually swarthy or ruddy, hands quite large with fingers that are not suited for detail work. Hair sandy or dark, becoming quite thin in the late thirties. The eye brows are heavy and there are likely to be found bumps on the head, moles and warts on some parts of the face.

The shorter persons of this sign make splendid business people, and have the talent for money-making to a large degree. They are somewhat headstrong, impatient of restraint or criticism, and utterly heedless of advice. They cut out their work for themselves, and insist on doing it in their own way. If this is not permitted — if they are interfered with, they frequentiy lose all interest in the subject at hand, and abandon it altogether. They are fond of planning, but dislike the task of working out details.

While there are differences of temperament between tall and short Aries people, they are all subject to the same mental influence, and many characteristics are common to both.

The Aries nature is strong and impetuous, with an inborn desire to command. Some of the world's greatest leaders have been born under this sign. Aries people have the utmost confidence in themselves and their ardent natures, overriding all obstacles, ignoring all opposition, and pressing onward to the desired goal even over the corpses of those who would stay their progress, makes it inevitable that their lives should be stormy and eventful.

They do not count the cost of success, and while they prefer honorable methods and pursuits, they will permit no considerations to outweigh their ambition. And they usually gain the reward they seek.

In their own strength and resourcefulness they can find no room for sympathy or pity for the weakness and failures of others.

Aries people, as has been said, are impatient of restraint, and absolutely incapable of being driven. But they can be led to loftier ideals by loftier natures, being readily responsive to good influences. At the same time they are equally responsive to influences of the opposite sort, and the very composition of their natures leads them often within reach of corrupting influences.

They have marvelously keen wit, ready and bright flow of speech, and pronounced convivial habits, and in congenial surroundings they are the leaders in social pleasures. As conversationalists they have few equals; never at a loss for subjects, nor for words in which to discuss them, they direct the flow of conversation into new channels, and furnish captivating entertainment for their companions, no matter of what class.

Aries people love harmony, order, and beauty in all forms. Their tastes are likely to be luxurious, and they are at their best amidst elegant surroundings.

They make excellent scholars in a general way, and what they learn they have the faculty of imparting to others. Literary pursuits are attractive to many Aries people, and from their ranks have come many eminent descriptive writers, poets, novelists and essayists, as well as teachers, public speakers, and actors. Lawrence Barrett, the great actor of serious roles, was Aries-born. It is also worthy of note that many high-salaried salesmen and buyers come out of this sign. They should devote considerable time to the study of occultism and like matters, and it is easily possible for them to develop marked powers of clairvoyance, telepathy, psychometry, etc.

The women of this sign, no less than their brothers, aspire to rule and to lead the van. It is not true that they do not know the value of money; rather they do not consider it, except as a means to an end. Consequently they are the greatest spendthrifts, simply throwing money right and left, in the desire to astonish or entertain or outshine others, so long as they can get hold of it. This desire to be considered leaders finds expression in their dresses, jewels and equipages, and in their demands for the best seats at the opera and good positions in any assemblage.

They insist on absolute independence in everything they do, and become unreasonably irritated at the slightest intimation of restriction or even disapproval. Their natures are perceptive rather than reflective, and their spirits delight in adventures.

People of this sign are instinctively loyal to their friends, in whom they can rarely see a defect. They will defend their friends with great vigor and fearlessness, just as they would defend themselves. They do not seek causes for quarrels, but their great courage and determination make them very much to be reckoned with when they do engage in any conflict.

They are very generous, but are not at all careful to discriminate between worthy and unworthy objects of their charity.

In delineating the characteristics of any class of persons, and in endeavoring to show them the paths of honor and success to which Astrology points, it is essential that they should be warned of the inherent elements of discord and evil in their natures. And so the Aries people as well as all others must be told of the faults and weaknesses that are likely to be theirs, and warned of the pitfalls they may encounter.

The principal defects in the character of Aries people are impatience, anger, selfishness, foolish generosity, and fickleness of purpose. They are not revengeful, but very slow to forgiveness. Egotism is another fault, and leads them sometimes to talk too much of themselves, their possessions and accomplishments. Jealousy, in Aries women, often mars what otherwise would be a most charming character.

Now in all this list of shortcomings there is not one that cannot be forever eliminated by the serious cultivation of the higher nature, and by permitting it to dominate the lower in every circumstance.

These people, as well as all others, must ever appreciate the fact that recondite or occult laws, magnetic currents and solar fluids constantly exert greater or less influence on the physical body, and that while these forces intensify the evil in lower or animal natures, they also impart power and vigor and health to those who seek to develop their higher selves.

So that in striving to eliminate their faults and to advance to the higher planes of life and conduct, the people of the earth are assured of the most powerful assistance, and they should invoke this assistance by rigorous self-communion, by constant efforts to give their better natures fuller sway, and by contemplation of the great truths of science and nature.

Aries people should cultivate patience. And by "patience" they should understand not only the capacity to await with composure for the working out of their plans, but the broader patience which bids us bear with the weaknesses of others, and with disappointments and vexations. This will prevent their fiery outbursts of anger and their intolerance of all who cannot agree with them.

The cultivation of the spirit of true charity will enable them to do good more wisely and will aid also in acquiring the virtue of patience.

Application they must learn, too, and concentration. "Keeping everlastingly at it brings success," and this means concentrated application of one's energy to one thing at a time.

Each day in the life of an Aries person should have a certain time, preferably soon after the noon-day meal, set apart for silent meditation on the serious subjects of life. This time should be given over to deep searching of the inner self, a calm appraisal of the tendencies to good and to evil, and to earnest effort to fix the mind unwaveringly upon the purity, truth and honor that leads to glorious heights. A solitary walk in pleasing, quiet places, where one will be free from distracting influences, will be found an excellent opportunity for meditation and self-communion.

The greatest power of an Aries person is to think. You throw your main dependence upon your head. Your fingers are too short and thick for fine detail work and furthermore your mind is entirely too active for two hands to carry out its dictation and hence you should be surrounded by a reliable staff of assistants to execute the details and bring to a successful completion your many undertakings. You are particularly adapted to the legal profession and would make an excellent claim agent for some large corporation, as you are a most capable adviser and can readily bring about a reconciliation with those where difference has arisen — and you have no doubt done this many times with your friends and associates.

The marriage of a person born under this sign is a precarious venture. Ideal companions though they are, in a general way, they know little of the more exalted phases of domestic affection. However, they are most likely to choose wisely if their choice of a life mate shall be one born under Sagittarius. Indeed, such marriages are usually productive of much happiness, and the offspring are vigorous mentally and physically. The marriage of one Aries person to another is also good, but the children are not so promising.

Children born under this sign are quite difficult to manage unless one has the key to their nature, which is reason, love and kindness. They are most sure to demand a reason and explanation at every turn. They are stubborn, self-willed and the best correction in the world for an Aries child is a calm and quiet talk at bed time. Corporal punishment is very harmful to these little folks and should seldom if ever be given, and then without anger. It is bad for many reasons, one is that it will require far more punishment to conquer them than their little frames can stand, another is that it will likely affect the brain and bring about serious troubles in the years to come.

As love is the only influence which can gain control over people of this sign, love should guide the hand and mind to which are entrusted the care of children born under Aries. Such children should never, under any circumstances, be coerced, tormented, scolded,

abused, or punished corporeally. **Kindness and gentle-**
ness must alone be employed in their government, **and**
they must be shielded from excitement and **every** untoward condition.

Aries people, young and old, should occupy **large**
and well ventilated sleeping rooms, with a constant
supply of pure, fresh air. For their best development
and health, they require an abundance of sleep. They
should eat regularly of plain, simple, nourishing food,
avoiding stimulants and repressing their inclinations toward high and luxurious living.

But these troubles are so generally the result of
disturbed mental conditions, due to worry, anger, jealousy, impatience, etc., that the way to avoid them is
very clear. Calmness, self-analysis and the complete
subjugation of the passions will enable Aries people
to become healthy, influential and successful in all they
undertake.

June and July are the most fortunate months for
people of this sign, preference being given to Tuesday.

Diseases invariably affect the head, headaches,
neuralgia, sunstrokes, affections of the eyes, ears
and teeth, and in case of fever which invariably
affects the brain. Stomach troubles, nervous prostration and paralysis. Any inharmonious condition that
should arise in the home and especially quarrels during the meal hours is most certain to result n sick
headaches.

Spacious rooms, harmonious surroundings, music
with abundance of rest and sleep is of untold value
to all Aries people. You are likely to suffer with
insomnia. You need little if any medicine.

Most all the diseases common to Aries people
are caused direct or indirect to overtaxing the brain.
Is it not advisable then that you should govern your
mental capacity strictly to the measure of your
strength. A walk, a drive into the country is the best
medicine in the universe, dear reader, and these lines
are well worth many times the price of the book,
if heeded.

You should never work late at nights, but should always arrange the greater tasks for the earlier part of the day.

If you will follow the teachings of Astrology you are sure of a speedy recovery in the event of any sickness.

This is but a chapter of your eventful life, Sir, so much has been said only to convince you of the real worth of the author and his wondrous work. I sincerely believe that I have given to the world a work that is worthy of the careful study of every thoughtful person in the universe.

You are a born ruler among men with a mind that is ever active, being earnest and sincere which inspires the confidence of all whom it is your pleasure to know.

It would be well for you to read carefully the contents on page 19 on special horoscopes.

LEO.

(July 22 to August 22.)

The sun, the source of all heat and light, is the governing planet in this sign, and as a consequence people born therein are remarkable in many ways.

In personal appearance they are, as a rule, of medium height, with strong, excellently proportioned bodies, broad shoulders, finely shaped heads, ruddy or light complexions, full and beautiful eyes, usually blue or hazel, strong, pleasant voices, with a quick and buoyant step.

They are warm-hearted, sympathetic, generous, magnetic, possessing highly emotional natures of great inherent goodness. Withal they are fearless and courageous, with strong intuition and remarkable insight.

These qualities are so closely intermingled with a philosophical, yet very practical nature that it will readily be understood that Leo people must be inevitably of strongly marked personality.

With proper training, they become the most skillful and efficient nurses in the world. Jean H. Dunaut, the originator and founder of the Red Cross Society, that famous organization that has brought comfort and courage and consolation to so many thousands of stricken humanity, was born under this sign.

With Leo people, impulse comes from the heart, not from the head, and they are manageable only by appealing to their love and sympathy. Argument and cold reasoning are useless to move them. Let impulse be coupled with their inborn courage and determination and they rush on to alarming extremes, unmindful of cost or consequences. Their quick intuition, however, may intervene to check their rashness before it is too late.

Under the benign influence of the true individuality of this sign, its people have high ideals and both inspire and entertain the most loyal love, pure, trusting and abundant. In their enthusiasm they create ideals which they are prepared to worship unstintingly and illimitably, and their affection survives any test except the great and inevitable one of the ideal. Brought face to face with reality and convinced of the falseness of the ideal they had erected, there ensues a brief but severe heartache, followed by a transfer of the affections to new objects, where love again flourishes with tropical intensity.

These people are born lovers, and can no more exist without sympathy and affection than a plant without water, light and warmth. If they do not get it from one source they will seek it elsewhere.

Their love is as loyal as it is intense. They resent a reflection upon the object of their regard with the utmost vigor. In fact, they are always fighting, or ready to fight, for those they love. To prove this statement, let the experimenter cast an aspersion upon a close friend or relative of a Leo person. The result will be highly and quickly convincing. And this defense of their loved ones has the further effect of increasing, if possible, their affection for the object of the censure or aspersion.

Of all people in the world, those born under this sign love amusement. It is the more dreamy, sensual sort that appeals to them, however, for they dislike physical exertion. Mental effort is equally distasteful, yet, despite this fact, their wonderful powers of intuition enable them to acquire knowledge, develop talent, and attain success in many fields of endeavor.

Leo people possess almost unlimited power to sway and inspire their fellow creatures. This faculty has made of them great generals, great orators and great actors. They climb to high places over the heads of their more tenacious and plodding fellowmen by sheer force of personality, good nature, and magnetism. Napoleon gave a striking example of this trait.

On the stage it is possible for these people to attain the highest rank — Mrs. Sarah Siddons and Mary

Anderson Navarro are examples. Their intensely
emotional natures, with their keen perceptions and in-
stinctive appeals to the inmost hearts of their audiences, give them the power to move them to trans-
ports of pleasure. Invariably, however, it will be found
that these Leo people act from intuition, and achieve
success without the long period of grinding study and
analysis that are necessary to less or differently gifted
natures. As a matter of fact, their aversion to study
any analysis is so strong as to make it actually out of
the question for them. Leo people seem to know things
without being taught, — without knowing themselves
how they know, and without being able to give ground
or reason for their knowledge.

In music also, they should find gratification and
success, combining brilliancy of technique with ready
inspiration. They should listen to much good music,
in any case, and if they have any talent in that direction, either for vocal or instrumental music, it will
be little less than a crime to neglect it. The same
rule will apply to any of the arts, or literature, or to
the more intellectual professions.

Leo people, when living under the influence of the
higher nature, have amazing power over the minds of
others. They may become powerful molders of public
opinion, — if they will but learn the pathway of silence
when silence is best. In general conversation, in rep-
artee, in story-telling, they are gifted far beyond the
average. They always make their own point, and are
equally sure and quick to see the points made by others.

Courage under adversity is one of the most marked
and admirable characteristics of the right-living Leo
nature. They do not care for detail; would much
rather plan work than execute it. In fact, they may
not be innocent of the charge of laziness, because they
love warmth and ease and indolence. Yet when adversity comes, when necessity arises, they display un-
bounded fortitude and inspiring courage, and do their
full duty promptly and effectively.

3

The people of this sign retain their youth and exuberance of spirit until well toward the end of earthly life. In many instances they really appear to grow younger as they become older.

These wondrous people have the greatest love for their own. In the rearing and management of their children they display great wisdom, and give no heed to the counsel of others. Mothers under this sign, who are paragons of gentleness and tenderness, will display the utmost ferocity if their children are injured or even reproved by others. They demand for all that is theirs the same measure of affection that is bestowed upon themselves. In homely phrase, their sentiment is "Love me, love my dog."

Planetary currents and solar fluids continually surround and permeate the people of this sign, and at times these mystic forces seem to illumine their personalities and cause them to seem possessed of supernatural power. These unseen forces, acting upon a mind rightly attuned and aspiring to pure and lofty attainments, confer immense possibilities for good, and make Leo people among the most talented, most blessed, and most lovable people in the world. Yet where the heart of the subject has not sought out the higher paths, — where the animal nature is in the ascendancy, these planetary influences are equally potent for evil. In short, they are strong weapons; their use for blessing or blasting must depend on the individual.

Undeveloped Leo people are possessed of many grave faults, all of which, however, may be removed. To no other class is it more important to overcome these flaws of character, because of the immeasurable happiness, honor, peace and love that will come when this is done.

Rashness, impetuosity, cunning, deceit, anger, vaulting ambition, and the passions of the flesh are the most pronounced of their defects. They must learn that their intuitions, (while it is true they are nearly always correct at bottom) must not be followed blindly. They must not jump at conclusions and act without further reflection. They must learn to curb their passions, especially that of affection for the opposite sex, and should spare no means to assure themselves by every possible test, that the object of their affection is worthy and honorable.

For ambition they should substitute the desire for the higher life of the spirit, lofty aims and pure individuality.

Many of the greatest and best people known in history have come out of this sign, and in all cases their greatness and goodness have been the outgrowth of their determination to overcome the grosser part of their natures and let the clear light of calm reason and the blessing of clean living claim full sovereignty.

In spite of their acknowledged courage, Leo people are subject to periods of depression and despondency. When these appear, let the person betake himself or herself to seclusion and quiet, and meditate on the great truths of Astrology and their bearing on his or her case. Let the faults and weaknesses be summed up and reviewed. Courage is there to look the facts in the face, and cheer is there in the knowledge that unseen, almost unknowable powers are ready to aid the subject to exercise his great will power, cast out all doubts and fears, and start anew with fresh resolves.

Do not dwell on the follies and shortcomings of others. Search out and destroy your own errors, that you may go forth to claim your rightful place among the most blessed of earth and carry hope and consolation and help to those who need them.

Those born under Leo see the light under most favorable auspices, and they should firmly grasp their great natural advantages. They can command and control the mysterious forces of the universe if they follow the plain teachings of Astrology, and do not dissipate and waste their energies, nor direct them to wrong designs. Thousands of examples prove that true happiness and prosperity can never come to Leo people until they learn how to control and dominate

their lower natures; but there is no limit to the wondrous things reserved for them when they once realize
and accept the better course mapped out for their
guidance.

In marrying, Leo people must exercise the greatest
caution and prudence. A mistake in this will lead to
a life of continual discussion and trouble. The step
should not be taken until well along in life, when the
character has become more settled and the spirit
molded into the likeness of goodness, charity and wisdom. Marriage with one from the sign of Sagittarius
(Nov. 22 to Dec. 21) or Aries (March 21 to April
19) is most free from objectionable tendencies, and is
quite likely to prove happy. The children of such a
marriage may be expected to be strong and healthy.

Children born under Leo are always extremely sensitive, passionate, self-willed, talented and imitative.
For this reason parents should strive to teach them
self-control, and at the same time set before them
always the best example of right living. These children require a strong hand to guide them and to
guard them from many evils and vices to which their
unawakened natures are prone. Their minds and hands
should be constantly employed with pleasant, whole-
some and useful tasks, and they require amusements
varied in nature and almost constant in supply. The
possibility of developing them into grand and noble
characters should impel their parents to every effort
to give them the proper training and restraint.

Leo people are so finely organized and so sensitive
that they often go through life without being understood and appreciated. Theirs is a love of sunshine
and shade, evolving into a sweeter, nobler purpose as
the shadows of life lengthen adown the wavering
landscape of time and melt at last into the twilight
of a dim eternity.

Weakness of the lungs, heart troubles, violent
fevers, affections of the kidneys and liver and back-
aches are the diseases mostly to be feared by Leo
people. However, all tendencies to disease and other

troubles may be counteracted and distress averted by following the teachings of Astrology.

Occupations. Designer, artist, cook, caterer, confectioner, actor, musician, house or floral decorator in which occupations you would likely excel.

You have an excellent memory and long remember an act of kindnees or ever grateful to those who have bestowed courtesies and the last to forsake a friend and a friendship once formed, you can rarely see a flaw — you are apt to go to the extremes of all things, love, hatred, appetites — passion, your sexual or love nature is usually strong, this one thing alone has been the rocks on which many beautiful lives of Leo people have been wrecked.

January and October are the most favorable months for people born in this sign, and Sunday the day of greatest pleasure and activity. They eagerly anticipate the coming of the sacred day, and sometimes endeavor to concentrate within its limits the energies of an ordinary week.

Leo people are honorable in their intentions, though frequently their natures are misunderstood. They find it far more agreeable to plan their work than the details involved in doing it.

The Sun being the governing planet of this sign, it is frequently found that they are greatly influenced by it, on the days when all nature is flooded with its golden rays. They are filled with confidence, light hearted and free from care, while on the days of cloudiness and gloom they lack confidence, push and energy to carry them on to success.

An entire volume could be written on the traits and characteristics of the beautiful sign Leo. There is no height too lofty for one of this sign to attain by right living and the guidance of one of the Author's Special Complete Horoscopes — see page 19, also the short talk on Sexology, page 118.

SAGITTARIUS.

(November 22 to December 21.)

In personal appearance people born under this sign are quite handsome. The eyes are a striking feature, being large and expressive, seeming to penetrate beyond the vision of ordinary mortals.

The taller and more slender ones are usually quiet, and strong intellectually. The shorter and more robust individuals are very graceful.

The Sagittarius people are entirely different from their fellowmen, and are truly remarkable in more than one respect.

Their talents and aptitudes are great and varied, and enable them to prosecute successfully many different enterprises and industries. In fact, many of the great achievements of the world are the work of people born in this sign, and they attain distinction, honor and wealth in numerous fields of accomplishment.

Business pursuits possess the greatest attraction for them, and they are happiest and healthiest when their affairs keep them busily employed. They have an enormous capacity for work, — so much so that to other people the extent of their energy and industry is incomprehensible.

Being gifted with truly remarkable foresight and keen intuitions, together with extreme carefulness for details, they are able mentally to work out their plans in advance and to forecast the progress and outcome of their projects and enterprises with remarkable accuracy.

This gift accords well with the fact that these people naturally belong to the domain of prophecy, and when spiritualized have considerable clairvoyant power.

They attend strictly to their own affairs, and are very likely sharply to resent any meddling, interference or even curiosity concerning them.

38

Their natures are strong, honest, **fearless and** blunt. They are neat and orderly in their habits, **and** appreciate these characteristics in others.

Their genius for business, their tendency to **keep** their affairs to themselves, their careful attention **to** details, and their keen foresight, naturally make them more than ordinarily successful, especially in financial matters.

They are not stingy, close or miserly; the facts are simply that they learn early in life to appreciate the value of money, and that habits of thrift and prudence are necessary if one expects to accumulate enough of this world's goods to insure a comfortable existence through life.

Their versatility also enables them to make money in dozens of ways, while other people are spending their time wishing for wealth.

Sagittarius people possess excellent judgment, and rarely make mistakes when they follow their own inspirations. Invariably, however, they meet with discouragement, and frequently with utter failure, when they permit themselves to be governed by the advice of others.

While they keep their own counsel concerning their own affairs, their goodness of heart and their generosity lead them to spur their friends on to success and share the rewards with them.

Very few men or women born in this sign are without means to provide for themselves in declining years. "To save is to have, and to have saved when you had," is Sagittarius' best judgment.

It follows that they are among the best financiers in the world, and that they are successful in any undertaking that involves the handling of money.

It must not be understood that they are in any degree sordid and grasping, bound up altogether in the pursuit of money.

Theirs is a noble and generous cast of nature, with minds preternaturally quick, an intense **love for truth** and an equally intense scorn for trickery and false ideas.

One of their most valuable traits is the quality of concentration. They do one thing at a time and do that one thing exceedingly well.

They cannot conceive that the truth can injure any man, and this belief, with their plain speaking, and the fact that they see things differently from most others, often causes them to give unintentional offense to their friends.

Sagittarius people are very magnetic and hypnotic, and their personality imparts to their words the power of striking deep into the hearts of their hearers.

Confining themselves always to the strict truth, their words have great effect. Some of the world's greatest leaders, teachers, speakers and reformers have come out of this sign.

Naturally happy and jovial in disposition, they are most acutely sensitive to appeals from the distressed and suffering, and their first impulse is to extend whatever relief is in their power. Often they are imposed upon, and the realization of ingratitude on the part of those whom they have aided hurts them deeply.

Although so reserved and secretive where their own affairs are involved, they abhor secretiveness in others, and are often opposed to secret organizations on this account.

This is an occult sign, and even to a greater degree a musical sign. Where the Sagittarius **person** has talent or inclination in musical directions it should be cultivated thoroughly.

Some of the world's most famous musicians are numbered among the sons of Sagittarius, a familiar and eminent example being Paderewski, the wonderful pianist.

The occultism of their characters makes it possible for these people to hear voices and behold visions that are beyond the ken of the world at large. The whole universe is open for the searching power of their minds, and their inner vision sees the truth more certainly and more quickly than does the ordinary mortal.

The women of this sign are skilled in all domestic affairs, are exceptionally good housekeepers, and display excellent taste in the arrangement and adornment of their homes.

The intensity of the Sagittarius nature tends to carry them to extremes in all things. Thus they are very good friends or very thorough enemies.

They are full of courage if required to act without reflection, but when given time for reflection are inclined to be timid and cautious.

They are naturally inclined to seek positions offering expansion and growth and freedom with honorable activity. They prefer always to associate with people in the higher walks of life.

As a rule they are fond of horseback riding, but should be exceedingly careful to avoid accidents that might occur in that exercise, as well as the danger of falling from great heights.

Travel especially appeals to them, and when they take vacations they are usually the occasions of long journeys.

In common with all humanity, the people of Sagittarius are subject to some faults and weaknesses. It is well for them to learn these things, because their innate nobility of character will lead them to try and eradicate them. They have a tendency to become unduly excited and angry over mere trifles. This they should avoid, and especially should learn to forget such things at once by dismissing them from the mind.

They must also learn moderation in their work. Their great energy begets impatience with ordinary methods, and their haste to accomplish results often leads them to sacrifice health and temper in the pursuit.

People born in other signs cannot comprehend the feverish activity that marks the Sagittarian, who frequently seem to expect others to be as active and energetic as himself. This is wrong. They must make allowance for the different tendencies and capacities of those not so highly organized as they are. This consideration will save them from much impatience and annoyance.

They should learn tolerance, gentleness in speech, and consideration for the feelings of others. We cannot all think alike, and it is well to recognize the fact that honest differences of opinion are bound to occur, and when they do, should be treated with courtesy and calmness.

They should not expect full appreciation for the good they do and the benefits they bestow. True gratitude is indeed rare; and they should learn that they may often receive ill returns for good deeds, and not permit such things to embitter their natures.

They should render themselves passively receptive to the wonderful planetary influences that will come to them in calmness and repose of spirit, bringing tremendous power and strength of character as well as true light and wisdom. When they can do this, they will eventually attain a high degree of perfection, and much peace and happiness will be theirs.

They should be careful in their choice of friends, and limit the number of those to whom they give their confidence. Thus they will avoid the risk of being misunderstood and save themselves from unkind criticisms and disappointment.

In selecting life mates, these people should be exceedingly careful, and endeavor to marry on the same intellectual and spiritual plane as themselves. They are naturally pure minded and abhor every suggestion of vulgarity, obscenity and licentiousness. In their marital relations they are the heart of constancy, and to be deceived embitters their whole existence, often leading to wild recklessness and dissipation that ends in death.

It is best for the Sagittarius person to marry one born in the sign of Aries (March 21 to April 19).

The children of such a union will be strong mentally and physically, and usually healthy and brilliant.

Happy, also, are marriages between two people born in this same sign, but the offspring are likely to be less strong and vigorous.

Much tact and diplomacy are necessary in governing children born under this sign. They must be made companions of their parents, and treated with confidence and trust.

They are unusually active, and must be given healthful occupation, which should be of their own choosing if this is practicable.

They are abnormally sensitive as well as wise and intuitive beyond their years. So they must be sincerely and tenderly loved and trusted, their confidence gained and never abused, and their wonderfully attractive natures allowed to develop in an atmosphere of kindness and gentleness.

They have universal love — the purest and noblest of earth, — and their affections are bestowed without discrimination. Particularly are they fond of other children, as well as of persons who are afflicted in some way, and this rare and beautiful affection should be nurtured and cultivated. Interference with this natural tendency may bring about most lamentable consequences.

February and June are the most successful months for Sagittarius people, and Thursday the day of the week to be given preference.

Summing up the study of the people of this sign, it will be seen that they are among the most charming and attractive personalities on earth, possessed of magnetic qualities of the highest order. The solar fluids and planetary forces that surround and permeate them are sources of strength and helpfulness.

Of course, not all of them have been awakened to the true light, and many of them, by living too deeply in the sensual part of their natures are depriving themselves of the glories and triumphs that might be theirs.

To all such it should only be necessary to show them the way of truth and light, and they may arise to grand and unlimited possibilities.

Your employers are fortunate indeed to have such as yourself in their services and no doubt have learned long ago that you was most faithful to every trust, your close attention to all details, strict practice of economy possessing as you do much mechanical ability. You execute an unusual amount of work with rare skill, there is a constant desire in your life to be ever active, in fact your health and happiness depends on activity, what you once learned, you have the faculty of retaining without difficulty, you surely cannot accomplish much under any feeling of restraint and in order to reach your highest accomplishments, you should be free and unhampered as you are deserving of the greatest trust and assuming great responsibility.

Rheumatism, weakness of the lungs and stomach trouble, are the diseases that affect the people of this sign.

The composition of your nature is so frank, earnest and outspoken that disagreements are likely to arise at any time, you are sure to utter the first thing that crosses your mind regardless of the views of others. You can't conceive why the truth should hurt any one.

You are a remarkable judge of character, being jovial, vivacious, combative and yet somewhat cautious and suspicious at times, especially so of strangers and when your suspicions are once aroused, you want to know the worst at the beginning, in fact it is quite impossible for one to deceive you. Should they succeed in doing so, they would not likely get a second opportunity.

At times you use poor judgment in your intense desire to be of assistance to those you love, and while your affections are deep and sincere, yet to many you appear outwardly, cold and reserved which

is apt to bring about social disagreements which is
sure to mar your life's happiness and you then would
suffer in silence.

Your generosity is often returned with ingratitude.
You are exceedingly fond of nature, hunting, fishing,
animals, flowers, etc. Not another person in any of
the Zodiacal signs can enjoy a good hearty laugh as
does those of this sign.

You have much musical, inventive, mechanical and
executive ability, as a cashier, ticket agent or any
position requiring quick mental calculations you would
excel. A full and complete Horoscope covering your
life would become of priceless value. See page 19.

GEMINI.

(May 20 to June 21.)

Well formed, handsome people, with clear eyes, bright complexions and a general appearance of vigor and strength, this description applies to the majority of persons born under the sign of Gemini — the Twins. These people have the strongest hearts of any of the people in the twelve signs of the Zodiac. Heart troubles are practically unknown to the people of Gemini.

The influence of this sign is apparent in the double nature of nearly all these people. With Mercury as your ruling planet, hence the unsettled conditions of both, mind and body, the eyes are rather small with a quick penetrating glance, usually dark or hazel, features small, nose and lips thin, long arms in proportion to body, hands and feet usually short and fleshy, high instep and found to be swift in all their movements.

The women of this sign are invariably of short stature, though graceful and active.

There are no members of the human race more generous, unselfish, affectionate and self-sacrificing and imaginative; none with stronger sympathies; none with higher capabilities of attainment when they have overcome the more earthly and animal parts of their nature.

The duality of their composition manifests itself in contradictory inclinations and desires, in restlessness, uncertainty, and discontent. They want to do certain things and at the same time they are almost equally desirous of doing just the opposite. They are not satisfied with things as they are, but cannot tell how they would wish to have them changed. They pray for riches and long life and almost in the same breath they say they care for neither.

These contradictory natures are nowhere else so clearly defined, and, in the undeveloped persons of this sign, they are the cause of much misery. The lower nature is indeed very low, while the higher goes just as far to the other extreme.

Until the higher nature is cultivated and developed to the utter destruction of the baser, Gemini people will suffer greatly in mind and body, and all these persons should learn this truth, and act upon it without delay.

As a rule, people of this sign are great seekers after knowledge, are omnivorous readers, covering extremely wide ranges in their reading, have very alert minds; and are excellent conversationalists.

The arts of handicraft appeals to them, and the nervous energy of their hands finds expression in transforming the creatures of their brains into realities.

Gemini persons have deeply religious characters, not confined to the beliefs of any particular creed or denomination, but extremely catholic in their tolerance and respect for all forms of belief and worship.

They have great pride of family, and this should spur them to earnest endeavors to make themselves worthy of their ancestry.

These people are the wanderers of the earth, and are exceptionally fond of sea voyages. Most of the romance, as well as most of the happiness of their lives, is likely to gather about their adventures by water, and especially in the South of France.

While the Gemini people are very sociable, they are ill at ease and uncomfortable in club or assembly life, which seems to sap their vim and personality. They cannot reach the same decisions, and agree upon the same lines of action, with their fellows. Argument and explanation are of no avail with them. Their general tendency is to disregard the usual customs which are accepted as good form.

In the case of Gemini people who have coarse hair and dark complexions, there is usually present a general state of combativeness, vague imaginings of evil,

and distrustfulness of others — even their usual associates.

They are not in any sense commercial and any attempt in that direction usually ends in disaster. They
are too generous and liberal to make any profit in business. If their scales showed 18 ounces they would call
it a pound and let it go, rather than seem grasping
and ungenerous.

As wage-earners they are not a success; they give
away their earnings as fast as they receive them, yet
they can and should learn moderation in this as in all
things else. They can and should learn provident and
thrifty habits, so that they can become capable money
earners and money savers, and at the same time have
more to give in sensible, true charity.

This thought will appeal to them, because of their
irresistible desire to help struggling humanity and
their kindly regard for the poor and needy.

People of this sign frequently display superior
executive ability with their hands. They can cut and
plan, and comprehend a device or pattern, and if not
interfered with will carry the work to successful completion, but they cannot tell in advance how it is to
be done.

They are very fond of the beautiful in nature and
art; with the women of this sign this is especially true.
To this characteristic we can trace their readiness to
make friends with people of handsome, easy and graceful appearance, regardless of deeper qualifications.

Having usually, brilliant and active imaginations,
Gemini people are often deep schemers; they readily
construct ideas and plots for novels and plays, and
their quick and restless minds find expression with
such aptness and rapidity as to astonish even themselves at times.

Some of the most famous wits in history were born
in this sign, as well as many highly gifted orators and
lecturers.

It will be understood from reading of their characteristics, that the unenlightened person of this sign is

likely to be possessed of many grave faults. These faults should give them deep concern, because, once they are recognized and admitted, half the battle for their extermination is won.

Gemini people — undeveloped — are suspicious, unreliable, untruthful and impatient. They are apt to be continually grumbling, growling and complaining, yet have no remedy to offer for the conditions of which they complain.

They imagine much evil, and are continually borrowing trouble. They assume to sit in judgment upon their fellows, and criticize them unmercifully for common weaknesses and frailties.

Serious and dangerous as are these faults of the Gemini nature, they are not by any means hopeless or helpless.

These people, consciously or unconsciously, are seeking repose and contentment. The only way in which they can attain these conditions is through the study of philosophy, religion, metaphysics and the occult sciences. All the evil tendencies we have enumerated will disappear when the higher nature begins to dominate.

One of the most important things to learn is to be thoroughly honest with one's self. With a full knowledge of his faults, a recognition of the misery they are sure to bring, and a firm determination to cast them out forever, the Gemini person can be assured of the final and complete victory of the spiritual over the carnal, and of illimitable and unceasing happiness, tranquillity and esteem.

Patience and silence must be the watchwords for those who have resolved to live on the higher plane. Patience with their fellowmen, silence as to their shortcomings.

It is well to admit that Gemini people go to one extreme or the other. They are either very successful and happy, or they have a very miserable existence.

4

Which shall be their lot depends altogether on themselves.

Majestic, mysterious and powerful magnetic and
planetary influences surround them always, available
for the greatest assistance in attaining the better mode
of life, or aiding the degraded soul to sink deeper and
deeper into the mire of misery and defeat.

In truth it must be said that the ordinary Gemini
nature is apparently shallow and superficial. Their inconstancy, their lack of continuity and fixed purpose,
their proneness to judge by appearances, their dissatis-
faction with the realization of their own desires, their
ceaseless activity, all these signs indicate a lack of
depth and stability.

Yet it is possible for all these weaknesses and defects to be overcome, and for the sons of the Gemini
to achieve distinction and power through careful cultivation of their better natures.

They should endeavor to associate with persons of
calm, thoughtful, self-contained habits, and should
earnestly strive to control their own restless selves,—
their hands, feet, minds and bodies.

With will-power and determination these wonderful influences may be drawn upon to serve the best
interests of the son of Gemini, and when this is accomplished, nothing good and desirable is beyond his
reach.

Gemini people seldom enter matrimony early in
life. Their nature is too variable — in youth the time
is occupied with knocking at so many doors they
haven't time to tarry at any one.

When they do marry it should be with those born
in Taurus (April 19 to May 20) or Aquarius (January
20 to February 19), and then there must be a liberal
supply of patience and a saving sense of humor on
both sides. These things will surely be needed.

Healthy and talented children are usually the fruit
of such unions. Gemini mates well, also, with Virgo.
(Aug. 22 to Sept. 23).

Children born in this sign require the very greatest care for their bodily and spiritual welfare. During the teething period they are likely to be subject to fits, and also to suffer from worms.

These children should be reared in an atmosphere of quiet and restfulness, and shielded from excitement and exciting scenes. They should be taught self-control early and in all things, — to eat slowly, and to yield themselves to authority. Their minds should be trained to resist the inclination to run riot and conjure up all sorts of evils. Teach them that their easily-aroused fears are groundless, and that nothing can harm them.

These little ones are most susceptible to affection, tenderness and gentleness, and should never be threatened or taught to fear anything but evil.

Gemini people are mostly liable to attack by throat and lung troubles, nervous prostration, and other nervous affections. Both old and young are often troubled with worms and eczema.

The women of this sign are frequently hysterical, due to their ill-balanced nervous composition.

What your nature lacks most is the power of concentration, learn to center your thoughts and energies on one occupation or profession, being unwavering, unflinching, fearless and deliberate, renewing your attack repeatedly until you have accomplished the end which you had set out for.

You are most enthusiastic in any line of thought in which you wish to take up, but in permitting your mind to relax, you again sink to the level from which you have arisen and all your efforts are again lost.

But by being persistent, each achievement won will strengthen the will-power and make it less difficult in the future — when you feel that restless desire for change coming over you, fight against it. It is only your lack of self-esteem and confidence that often retards your progress.

April and August are the most fortunate months for Gemini people with preference given to Friday.

If you will properly fill out the coupon after carefully reading the contents of pages 19, 20 and 21 and mail it to the Author, you will receive much valuable advice in a more detailed Horoscope, entirely devoted to the sign Gemini.

LIBRA.

(September 23 to October 23.)

This sign indicates impartial justice, absolute fairness, rare good judgment, and a fine liberality of thought.

People born in this sign are usually tall and well-formed, inclining to slenderness. Their faces are oval, their mode of speaking quick and decisive, and their movements graceful and alert. They are very careful of their personal neatness and cleanliness, and greatly dislike hard and dirty work. Libra's most marked characteristic is keen foresight, exceedingly positive and decisive in all undertakings. They should execute their own ideas as they were originally planned, for the reason that they are susceptible to the minds of others.

The people born in this sign are qualified above all others, to fill worthily positions of authority, where they may be called upon to decide the affairs of others.

They are born leaders of mankind, holding their power over their fellows by sheer force of unassailable right, and meeting successfully the severest tests to which their pre-eminence exposes them.

Justice, strength and liberty are the guiding influences in their lives, and the true son of Libra never misuses the immense powers that are bestowed upon him at his birth.

Their minds are largely original in their operation, and their ideas too far advanced to permit them to rest content in subordinate places. They cannot successfully carry out the prearranged plans of others, in the making of which they have not had a large part, and their attempt to do so brings only disappointment.

They have the capacity for doing great things, but must do their work in their own way.

In affairs of state, in international matters of state-craft, and in all relations where supreme clearness of mind and purity of purpose are demanded, Libra men are distinguished for their ability. President Hayes and many other eminent statesmen came out of this sign.

This sign probably has produced more famous actors and actresses than any other one in the Zodiac. Sara Bernhardt, Mme. Modjeska, Peg Woffington, E. H. Sothern and many others are from Libra.

They always attract a numerous and loyal follow-ing. The splendid magnetism, precision of thought and decisive action compel unhesitating allegiance, even in the face of strong opposition.

People born in Libra have deeply intuitive percep-tions which seem to enable them to read the deepest consciousness of their associates and all with whom they come in contact.

They literally "feel" truth or falsity, affection or aversion, and are more likely to be influenced by the unexpressed thought of others than by utterances of speech.

They are extremely approachable, and are never "too busy" to give consideration to those who seek them. They hear each man's plea with impartial pa-tience, carefully weigh all the factors in the case, and from the depths of their profoundly judicial natures they speak the truth as it appears to them.

If they err at all in their conclusions, it is always in the direction of leniency and charity for the frail-ties of their fellow men.

They love humanity for itself alone, and because of the measureless sympathy of their temperaments. For the afflicted and distressed, for the worthy unfor-tunate, no matter how lowly, they display the utmost tenderness; and their goodness does not content itself with mere expressions of sympathy.

Any worthy cause or individual appeals to them so strongly that they do not hesitate to make great per-sonal sacrifices in order to be of practical assistance.

Those born in this sign, especially the women, possess souls so finely sensitive to harmony and inharmony that they instinctively recognize the one or the other as existing in any environment they may enter.

The effect of inharmonious conditions upon them sometimes causes them to seem sorrowful or disturbed or indifferent, giving color to the charge that they are disagreeable and inconstant. Such conditions subdue their high spirits and reflect a shadow upon their companions.

It being impossible for them to conceal the effect of their inward feelings, and equally impossible or inadvisable to explain the reasons, they prefer silently to suffer the unkind misjudgment of others.

Tenderness of heart is a marked characteristic of this sign. They have an innate horror of blood and cruelty, and are much distressed to know of brutal, inhuman treatment of dumb animals. Frequently it is found that the women of this sign cannot ever bear with composure the sight of chicken killing.

The men are very self-reliant, seeking their own companions, amusements and occupations. Very frequently they learn to make working capital of their inspirations and considerable clairvoyance, in such cases often becoming speculators, stock brokers and even gamblers.

As a rule the men are of fascinating personality, especially to those of the opposite sex. They are quite apt to be reckless in the pursuit of pleasure and in gratifying their desires, just as they are when engaged in speculation or gaming.

They are always hopeful and strong, recovering quickly from reverses or disappointments, so that losses and disasters do not affect them deeply.

Libra women are a little more cautious than their brothers, but are prone to carelessness in financial affairs. They do not care for the details of money matters, and really prefer not to be bothered about such things.

With all the keenness of their sense of justice, they cannot understand why one from whom they may borrow money should be at all disturbed or annoyed by their failure to repay it at the time agreed upon.

This peculiarity does not arise from the slightest intention to defraud. These people are the soul of generosity. The larger half of anything they have to divide always goes to the other party, but the son of Libra would not expect the same treatment were he the receiver and some one else the divider.

Libra people seem irresistibly attracted toward the busiest throng, and they enjoy visiting the halls of justice, the theater and other places where people congregate.

On the lower plane of life, Libra people, by their recklessness, impatience and dissipation of vital forces, make themselves liable to serious disorders of the digestive organs, and to nervous prostration and similar affections. Immunity from these troubles, and from all others, will come to them when they have found the true way and walk therein.

They are sometimes very impatient and this causes them to lose much of their vital force. Strange as it may seem, with their admirable composition, they easily become confused. They are nervous and excitable over so familiar an act as crossing a crowded thoroughfare. Careless of their belongings, also, they often misplace or actually lose things.

Enveloping and investing these people are the most wonderful magnetic forces, which impart animation and vigor to them. Their natural ability to acquire occult powers and intuitive knowledge is often phenomenal. With their exceedingly rare and keen perception, there is no human attainment beyond their capacity if they become spiritualized.

Libra people, in view of their remarkable natures and immense possibilities, should earnestly undertake to comprehend their own natures, to develop their higher tendencies, and completely to annihilate the ignoble and baser characteristics that too often accompany this sign.

Their chief fault, perhaps, is the tendency to be too strongly attracted by the material side of life. When they have been brought to realize that their only hope of true happiness and prosperity lies in yielding to the dictates of the higher consciousness and denying the claims of their lower tastes and desires, they become the most loyal and lovable friends, husbands, wives and parents.

In the very openness and generosity of their dispositions, these people often waste their powers and strength, dissipating their forces broadcast. Desiring to help all humanity, and to do it at once, they fail to perceive that in order to be really helpful they must first learn to husband their own strength and resources.

They are inclined to be egotistical, vain and proud, and to place undue value upon the applause and approbation of the multitude. They cannot brook criticism, even though they know it is just.

Intuition often tells them when they are the subjects of unfavorable or unfriendly thought in the minds of others, and this knowledge makes them miserable.

While they do not become angry very often, when this does occur, it is cyclonic in its fury, and from its evil effects they do not recover for a long time.

Their excess of enthusiasm frequently leads them to exaggeration, which, while not so reprehensible as wilful untruthfulness, should be carefully avoided.

Trifling affairs, or absolutely no consequence sometimes cause them deep distress. Their feelings are easily hurt, or perhaps it is truer to say that their vanity is easily wounded.

For the removal of all these weaknesses the Libra people should spend some time daily in seclusion, where they may meditate deeply upon their own character and form high resolves for better living. Patience, humility, repose, self-control, purity of thought and deed should be their constant aim and desire.

They should, in their spare time, devote themselves to the study of art, literature and the occult sciences or metaphysics.

Music is a powerful agent for good to the Libra nature, and every musical tendency should be carefully and persistently cultivated. The influence of good music, even where the Libra person is sunk in the depths of sensuality, will often inspire them with better impulses and raise them to the point where they can see and realize the better things of existence.

Libra is distinguished from the other eleven signs of the Zodiac in that it is the only one that is characterized by three distinct and differing types of personality, each one of these types possessing peculiarities and tendencies which make it quite unlike the other two.

In one of these types the subject has a straight, narrow forehead, and the strongest trait of this type is an unusually fine judgment in commercial and mercantile affairs. These people display remarkable foresight, apparently; as a matter of fact, it is their great power of intuition that serves them so well. They excel as buyers; they seem accurately to forecast the probable demand for goods, and a merchant of this type is very rarely found with an overstock of goods in any particular line. They are able to form excellent opinions as to the probable extent to which any deal may profitably be carried, and seldom overestimate their own capacity for handling such deals. As salesmen, also, they are without superiors, their intuition helping them to gauge the inclinations, tastes and temperaments of their customers and so to advance the proper arguments to bring about the sale.

Another type of the Libra sign is marked by a rather receding forehead, and, in the language of phrenology, they have well developed powers of perception and, usually, a large degree of conscientiousness. These persons are best adapted for speculative pursuits. They should restrict their dealings to "short turns"; that is, to such articles or commodities as can be bought and sold quickly, and that will not require to be carried on hand or kept in stock any length of time. In short, they should always try for "quick action." The intuitive faculty is very marked in all people born in Libra, but the people of this second type are peculiarly gifted with ability to discover defects and weaknesses instantly. They are indeed seldom deceived when they trust to their own individual judgment. If they will cultivate moral habits of life these people will always have plenty of money.

In the third class of Libra people, the heads are much broader through the temples and the foreheads are well rounded. Those of this type are better fitted to become expert accountants and bookkeepers. They have a natural inclination to acquire several languages, and should be able to hold good positions as interpreters and foreign correspondents with exporting concerns. They possess inquisitive minds, and are always interested in closely examining every sort of intricate or ingenious device they may encounter. They are fond of scientific learning, and their libraries usually comprise numerous volumes on such subjects. The greatest natural mechanics in the universe are found in this class of Libra people, and the higher the development of their inherent talents the greater success they will achieve. The author's researches among the records of those of this type have disclosed the fact that many eminent actors, orators, and authors have been in this class.

A Libra person should *never* contract marriage with one born under Pisces (February 19 to March 21) yet strange as it may seem, Pisces usually selects Libra for a partner in a matrimonial attempt. The two natures are absolutely incompatible, and their union is invariably attended by distressing results.

Pisces always insists on knowing the whys and wherefores; must be given reasons for every action, motive, deed. Libra cannot give these reasons and does not think it worth while to try, consequently quarrels and turmoil are naturally the outcome. Virgo

(August 22 to September 23), is almost as unsuitable as Pisces as a mate for Libra.

On the other hand, the union of Libra and Sagittarius (Nov. 22 to Dec. 21) is certain to be happy, (other things being congenial), and the children are sure to be talented. Children of Libra and Aquarius (Jan. 20 to Feb. 19) are strong and possess keen intellects.

When children are born under Libra their management, training and education are matters of grave moment. Great patience and care are indispensable.

These children are either very good and true, or the exact opposite. Parents are often astounded at the sayings and doings of these little ones. As a matter of fact, they are very susceptible to psychological influences, and are scarcely to be held to account for their peculiarities.

They should early be taught the fundamental truths of nature, especially those of the function of generation, and should not be deceived by prudish or conventional instructions.

Tenderness, gentleness and patience must be exercised in correcting them when this is necessary, and they are generally amenable to such methods.

They have natural inventiveness and much originality, and often more real knowledge than their parents. They give utterance to the most unexpected thoughts, and it is always best to listen to them with loving attention. Ridicule or laughter often drives them to deception.

August and December being the more fortunate months with preference given to Friday.

You are a skilled mechanic in any line, your plans have been most carefully laid and are executed with indifference as to the opinions or suggestions of others and you are willing to resume all responsibility that might arise.

Your great personal magnetism and honest dealings make you most worthy and well liked by all.

See special note on Sexology, page 122.

AQUARIUS.

(January 20 to February 19.)

"Fight on, Aquarius, in the world's battles, and conquer all."

Out of this sign come the very strongest and the very weakest people in the world. They can achieve the best and highest things, or they can be utter failures. And it lies with themselves to say and prove to which extreme they will go.

Birth in this sign indicates a noble and progressive nature, and a quick, receptive mind, with more than a touch of genius, inclining to the fine arts.

Some very famous and greatly revered names appear on the roll of the Aquarius-born. Mendelssohn, the master-mind among the world's composers, whose wedding march has lent its wonderful harmonies to uncounted thousands of nuptial scenes throughout all Christendom, from palace to cottage, and whose Spring Song has been chosen for rendition at the most brilliant functions prepared by social leaders; Mozart, scarcely less gifted than Mendelssohn; Robert Burns, the well loved poet of Scotland; the brilliant Byron, one of the most talented of poets; Abraham Lincoln, and as well, that great statesman and president, Wm. McKinley, whose last earthly words were "It is God's way"; these are but a few of the many notable sons of this sign who are deep in thought and sparing in speech.

Men born under Aquarius attain to great things, and the fulfillment of their still greater promise is defeated only by the leisurely habits which characterize most of this sign.

They dream of magnificent achievements, but find the dreaming much easier than the accomplishment. The thought of heroic deeds to be done stirs their

61

imaginations, but seldom imparts the requisite activity to their natures to make the thoughts become realities. Their minds paint many a picture that their hands do not transfer to canvas, or plan many a castle that may never reach completion.

They seldom assume leadership. It is only their inherent dignity (which they never forget) and excellent reasoning faculties that impel them to push their reforms and purposes in a quiet but persistent and logical manner, reaching their fellowmen, and stirring their impulses, by the pen rather than by speech. Although they are brilliant writers they are not often clever conversationalists, seeming to lack that personal magnetism and dramatic manner of easy poise that compel effective attention.

The depth of their natures precludes much surface indication of what may be passing within them. Like running water, the shallow murmurs and babbles as it passes on its way, while the deep goes on in tranquil silence.

The men born in this sign not only buoy up the hopes and aspirations of others, but discover in them unsuspected stores of good, which they bring to fuller realization by imparting self-confidence and ambition to accomplish better things than may have seemed possible.

Naturally they are oftentimes cruelly disappointed by those who have profited by their generosity, and who are utterly unable to appreciate true worth, nobility and unselfish greatness.

Yet these disappointments seldom provoke either bitterness or complaint from the Aquarius person. They merely retire more closely into their own consciousness and understanding, finding adequate consolation and comfort there.

Those born in this sign are inclined toward conditions of gloom, the contentions about them breeding a melancholy fondness for the solitary places of earth. They are attracted to lonely lakes and glens, to historic ruins, and places of that character. Many an Aquarius-born person is drawn as if by supernatural agencies to the time-stained edifices of Trinity and St. Paul's churches, and to the quaint old tombstones marking the resting places of the quiet dead, within sound of the rush and roar of Broadway.

This same preference for moodiness and sombreness pervades their taste in art. They prefer the darker, more grewsome and uncheerful products of the painter's brush. In their dress, too, they are often known to adopt these darker, more obscure shades with such excellent effect as to arouse frequent comment on their "perfect costumes."

Yet they do not wish to appear conspicuous for their superiority in dress, but would be glad to have all their friends and companions receive the same compliments that are given themselves.

Aquarius people are the personification of dignity and are never found mixed up in vulgar brawls and dissensions.

They are very intuitive, unusually clear reasoners and remarkably fine judges of character, especially where matters of honor or dishonor are involved. Their minds are very active in planning for and promoting the good of all the people — the general public.

They possess a great deal of psychic ability or controlling power of the eye, and minds that are keen and admirably adapted to pleasing the masses.

They are invariably faithful to their duties and to trust reposed in them in whatever sphere they may be called to occupy.

The women of this sign are very loyal, faithful and devoted wives, with minds of striking purity and nobility.

Aquarius people should avoid all legal complication and entanglements, since they invariably suffer injustice and unfavorable verdicts. Many an honest man born in this sign has been unjustly deprived of his liberty or property, for the baleful influence of Saturn, the evil planet, rules people born at this time.

They are also liable to suffer from accidents on the water — by ocean, river or lake travel.

Their temperaments are nervous, and they have a natural tendency to nervous disorders, rheumatism, pains in the head and feet, impaired circulation, brain troubles, loss of vitality, melancholia, despondency, etc.

They are not rote students, usually lacking the concentrative power so essential to effective study. Yet they seem to absorb information from every source, without apparent effort.

Aquarius people are always agreeable and courteous, rarely passionate or quick-tempered, but preferring and practicing calmness and peacefulness. At the same time they recognize insult or indignity when it is offered, and know how properly and fully to resent it.

Some very famous financiers have been born under Aquarius, but to succeed in amassing wealth, one of this sign must cultivate self-reliance and learn to depend altogether on his own powers. Too often they are timid and half-hearted in pushing their enterprises, and this results in failure or disappointment.

Aquarius people are naturally endowed with great possibilities, and are subject to wonderful planetary influences. When these things are understood and appreciated, and the beneficent powers invoked, these people can rise to supreme heights of strength and usefulness. Even when only partially aware of their natural gifts, they can succeed in almost any field of endeavor.

When these people realize their higher nature and strive to live in the eternal they are very honest, gentle, kind-hearted, active, industrious, shunning debt, and becoming, as they should, the strongest of the strong. Some of the greatest spiritual healers ever known came from this sign, and, as a matter of fact, every one born thereunder is a natural healer, although very few of them are aware of it.

Aquarius people should learn at once to develop their rare gifts and powers. To do this they should seek to understand wherein their natures are defective, and urge themselves constantly upward to the light and away from the side of darkness, unbelief, and the grosser things of earth.

They must firmly believe in themselves, and that they are vastly worth while in the scheme of life. Yet they must not go to the other extreme, as do so many who are unawakened, and set too much value upon public opinion, thereby becoming mere weak time servers.

They must learn to keep their own affairs to themselves and not talk too freely concerning them. Having mapped out their course, they should stick to it with the greatest determination and let nothing swerve them.

The most prominent faults and weaknesses of this sign are indolence, proclivity to disregard promises, vacillation, caprice, uncertainty, lack of hope, procrastination, boasting and loud talking.

All these things are evidences that the person is permitting the evil tendencies of the Aquarius nature to dominate, and many of the faults enumerated are but different manifestations of the same tendency.

All can be overcome, and must be overcome before the Aquarius person can hope to realize the slightest measure of the true joys of existence.

Unawakened people of this sign are continually seeking advice on all sorts of subjects, but never accepting or acting upon it, however good.

They ask questions with the utmost apparent desire for enlightenment, but straightway forget the answers.

Practice of self-reliance will do away with these habits, and with the consequent vacillation of purpose and lack of concentration.

Work and plenty of it is the best thing for these people. Very few of them are mechanics, yet they possess considerable ability in this line.

5

They must be optimistic, and seek for the good that is in all things, turning away from the darker side of life.

They should not concern themselves about the frailties and faults of others, nor permit themselves to become unkind critics.

Two excellent mottoes for those born in this sign are "Mind your own business" and "Business before pleasure."

Punctuality and promptness, also, must be learned and practiced unremittingly.

When the higher nature is awakened in the Aquarius born, and they are aroused to work for righteousness, improvement is rapid, and the encouragement that enters their souls carries them on to blessedness undreamed of before.

All persons born in this sign have the gift of the spirit, and should they choose to recognize and employ it they are very wonderful indeed.

The eyes of the silent, quiet, dignified Aquarius person have great hypnotic force, and when the light that shines from them is that of the spirit, the ability to heal and comfort is almost superhuman.

Social and business affairs will yield the greatest enjoyment and profit, and every task becomes a pleasure, when the Aquarius person is associated with one born under the sign of Gemini (May 20 to June 21). The reason for this is found in the congeniality of the Gemini temperament, with its sudden inspirations, fearless actions, and swift soaring fancy, which are a source of perpetual delight to the eager minds of the Aquarius-born.

Marriage relations between Aquarius and Gemini should prove a pathway of flowers, replete with peace, happiness and contentment.

Children born under this sign are very finely organized and under proper treatment will develop into noble men and women. They will invariably reflect the spirit in which they are met. For truth and gentleness they will return truth and gentleness; for cruelty and doubt they will return cruelty and doubt.

They have splendid memories, and they do not soon forget either good or bad.

They should be surrounded by loving, truthful and congenial companions and guarded from confusion and excitement.

Restless and impatient, they require a great deal of out-door exercise and suitable amusements. Country life is best for them, and they should never under any circumstances be compelled to attend school against their will.

While you are exceedingly loyal to your friends, yet there is a tendency for you to be careless in keeping you appointments — in short you are somewhat of a promise-breaker.

You have the faculty of explaining a subject so that it is most easily comprehended by others. Your arguments too are most convincing and go straight to the heart of your subjects. Excellent sentiments, natural gift of speech which makes you well fitted to public life, you are a natural salesman and would be particularly successful in all financial matters, though apt to be lacking in self-confidence, as a promoter for corporations or any large schemes, you are well adapted.

The silent hypnotic eye of an Aquarius person is most fascinating and bewitching, while the expression upon the face is that of an inquiring one, the eye being so accurate, the judgment so keen, that they may safely be trusted to size up a person's honesty at a single glance. Are always of a robust, healthy appearance. Seldom of short stature.

Some of the greatest men in the world's history was born under this sign. You too, can rise if you get the right start. Astrology points the way, and nature does not discriminate. Remember sir, that the world's greatest men came from the ranks of humble homes. My special Horoscope is for the man with a purpose. See page 19.

April and August are most favorable for Aquarius people, and Saturday the best day of the week.

TAURUS.

(April 19 to May 20.)

This nature is born to a heritage of strength and freedom, storm and stress. It brooks no fettering impediments. Its God-given capacity for great things must have full scope to seek unlimited, unhampered development.

It is an excellent birth sign, bestowing upon its proteges a wealth of sterling attributes than can scarcely fail of the highest success.

Those born under this sign are for the most part, are of a robust healthy appearance, with full faces, thick neck and lips, wide nose and mouth, florid complexion or a smooth shiny skin, a broad thick short hand, large frames and broad shoulders, representing studious, labor, will and endurance.

This type of physique is most excellent, giving promise of youth, vigor and freshness, even far into the declining years of life.

They are light hearted and of joyous spirits, and sorrow passes them lightly by. Country life has strong attractions for them in their seasons of relaxation and recreation, although they almost invariably make the city the scene of their work and their homes.

Taurus people are blessed with very strong, active brains, and are likely to be diligent students and to acquire superior educational attainments.

Their minds are probably the most receptive in the world, and they easily assimilate the thoughts of others. At times it is quite difficult for the Taurus person to distinguish clearly between the conceptions which have originated in his own mind and those which he has unconsciously absorbed from the minds of his associates.

Literary pursuits possess strong attractions for many

people of this sign, and their studious habits give them considerable ability in this direction. At the same time they are likely to be more imitative than imaginative or creative.

Their power of memorizing is very great, enabling their minds to retain details and particulars of innumerable subjects with surprising accuracy and ease.

A liberal endowment of self-reliance gives them admirable courage, and an intuitive ability properly to gauge public opinion qualifies them to succeed extremely well in the field of politics and finance. Some of the world's most influential and able politicians and public men have come out of this sign.

As a rule, when they become politicians or office holders they are of the better sort or more faithful class. An absolute reverence for confidence reposed in them is one of the strongest and most admirable characteristics of the Taurus-born.

This qualification is also of vast value to them when they take up financial pursuits. Many of the most honored and successful bankers were born in this sign, and their excellent judgment and steady persistency, with unwavering fidelity to every trust, win them impregnable positions in the esteem of their fellow men.

They are very magnetic, and hence well liked by every one. The number of their friends is limited only by the number of their acquaintances, and they find much pleasure in the knowledge of these friendships.

These people are seldom talkative. Their knowledge and intuition lie deep and do not readily appear on the surface, but people of less depth and strength of character soon learn to rely for mental and moral advice and encouragement upon these sturdy sons of Taurus.

While they possess undoubted talent in finance, and are almost sure to succeed in such matters, they do not attach to money any special value except as a means of doing good.

They do not find it difficult to accumulate money, but they rarely hoard it, being always ready to share it with less fortunate people.

Their generosity of spirit **prefers** to make itself evident in the very practical form of money rather than in kindly but ineffective expressions of sympathy.

They take immense delight in the pleasures of the table. The good things of life are for them almost the chief end of existence. In those pleasures also, their generous nature prompts them to share with others; and they are never more happy than when they are able to spread bounteous feasts before their friends.

This fondness for good eating and drinking is not the only tie that binds the Taurus person to material pleasures. Their whole natures are inclined to purely physical enjoyment of all forms, and they display as much persistency and determination in the pursuit of such entertainment as in the more commendable things of life.

They have remarkable powers of concentration, and are imbued with magnetic and sympathetic forces that make them excellent mental healers.

Taurus people come into the world during the mating season, naturally they have the strongest wills, appetites and passions of all the signs. Taurus boys and girls are more apt to make a hasty marriage, or wreck their beautiful lives in personal excesses. They are at all times in such close harmony with nature that their senses are ever active and they truly enjoy a sensuous existence.

While they are so strong of will and so finely equipped mentally, they are easily controlled through their sympathies when it is possible to arouse them. The youth of this sign, particularly, are easily led by such means, — often to their sorrow.

Taurus people are the most loyal of friends, but must be permitted to have their own way and to dominate the friendship. When they become enemies their enmity is as thorough as their friendship, nor do they easily forgive or forget.

Their tendency to generosity and practical sympathy often leads the Taurus people to take upon themselves an overload of the sorrows and burdens of others.

In a nature marked by so many positive characteristics as that of the Taurus, it is inevitable that there should be great possibilities for the highest good, and equally great possibilities for the grossest evil.

In the wonderfully attractive, magnetic, loving and lovable people of this sign, there are certain tendencies toward debasing habits and modes of life, which may be removed and destroyed with the happiest results, but which, if allowed to continue and to dominate, will inevitably bring sorrow and misery and distress upon the subject.

Their animal natures being so highly emphasized from birth, the Taurus people should exercise every means to bring it under full and complete control.

Its very strength and fullness and vigor, when properly controlled and directed, is the means of making these people immeasurably powerful for good. They can rule and righteously govern great bodies of men; they can acquire extraordinary psychic energy; they can become wealthy to any extent they desire, they can become models and symbols of dignity, courage, purity, loyalty and personal excellence.

Control of the passions, then, is the most important task that can engage the mind of any one born in this sign.

Undeveloped Taurus persons are the most headstrong, unreasonable people on earth. They demand their own way in all things and opposition or resistance arouses them to almost demoniacal outbursts of anger and violence.

In these fits of passion they sometimes appear to be actually insane, and in truth are dangerous to live or associate with, being utterly irresponsible. They rave and rant, and wreak their anger on whatever may stand in their path, whether it be inanimate objects like furniture or the very person of whom they are most fond when calm and in their right minds.

They are not only unreasoning, but absolutely unmanageable when passion assumes its unbridled sway, and there is nothing to be done except to leave them

alone — literally — until their violence has spent itself
and reason has returned.

In the lower types of this sign there is a domineering spirit which makes them very much disliked. Such
persons are very arbitrary and exacting, and insist on
either ruling or ruining. The lot of the wife of such
a man is likely to be a most cruel one, filled with
sadness, misery and physical terror.

Ardent, passionate and impetuous by nature, the
salvation of these people lies in acquiring mildness
and gentleness, consideration for others, and the most
rigid self-control and self-discipline.

The Taurus nature, when awakened, may be com-
pared to a mighty locomotive, capable, under intelligent
control, of performing its appointed work with speed,
certainty and dignity, but capable also of spreading
death and destruction in its terrible path if it escapes
the vigilance of the guiding intelligence.

Until Taurus people learn to respect themselves, by
respecting others, they are continually miserable and
often dangerously ill. They are subject to the most
horrible fits of depression, and to heart troubles, dropsy
and tumors.

These ailments result from the improper dissipation
of the immense vitality nature gives the Taurus people.
They are prone to give unbridled license to all their
appetites; they eat too much, their food is too rich,
and they make no attempt to curb or restrain the carnal passions.

Self-control then in the very broadest and most
comprehensive interpretation of the term, must be the
first and unwavering aim of the Taurus person who
aspires to secure the full enjoyment of the high possibilities which planetary influence would bestow upon
his life.

With self-control, all the evil passions and tendencies, together with their terrible consequences, will be
overcome, and the really fine and lovable character of
this sign will shine forth in all its destined beauty and
vigor.

They should be alone a great deal, and in calmness and meekness of spirit seek to know their real natures, and to permit the desire for the higher life to enter in and dominate their souls.

They should avoid too much stimulating food and alcoholic drinks. They should also school themselves to look upon members of the opposite sex with pure minds. Over-exertion, which entails increased heart-action, is quite dangerous for people of this sign.

Patience and silence will do much for the Taurus person who seeks the light.

The women of this sign make the most devoted and constant wives, and will willingly endure the greatest privations and make the greatest sacrifices for those they love. They should always be on their guard against insincere sympathy and evil-minded flattery. Their kindly, sympathetic natures make them very susceptible, and unless they are very careful they may be led far astray.

All people born in this sign would find it a wise plan to make all decisions of any moment when alone and free from interference, influence or excitement. If they do this, their decisions are much more likely to be according to their own judgment, which is usually excellent.

On awakening in the morning, the work of the day should be planned and conclusions and decisions made, as far as possible, and then adhered to throughout.

The happiest marriage for one born in Taurus will be when the mate is of the sign of Capricorn (December 21 to January 20). Next in desirability would be one from Libra (September 23 to October 23). When the marriage is with other signs than these, the children are likely to die in infancy, and the union is an unhappy one in most respects.

These Taurus folks are, when living on the higher plane, the practical, useful dependable people of the universe, worthy of all honor and trust. While they demand the greatest liberty to do things in their own way, they have the confidence in themselves that carries them through to victory where defeat might await one of inferior courage. The world makes way for him who knows where he is going; and the Taurus person, once started, is never in doubt as to his goal.

Children born in this sign are sturdy, passionate little creatures, and the effort to develop their wills along right lines, and to teach them to be masters of themselves, should be begun early. They are usually voracious eaters, and inclined to be cruel to animals. Both these tendencies may be overcome with care and tact, since the children may be calmly reasoned with and led through their better natures, whereas it would be folly to try to drive them against their wills.

These young Taurus persons should have the best educational facilities and should be encouraged by every means to take advantage of them. Proper education will be much needed in the struggle they must inevitably meet in life.

You have much executive ability, are patient in details and capable of carrying to a successful issue the gigantic plans of others, as a contractor and builder you would likely excel, having the faculty of taking up the most complicated plans of others and place them into actual operation, your unyielding determination and strong will-power enables you to succeed in many branches of industry. Your tastes artistic — your observation most keen.

While you are strong intellectually and equally as strong in appetite and passion, these two monsters have been the hidden reefs which have wrecked what would otherwise have been a most happy and successful career. Through right though and proper living you could succeed in almost any undertaking, if you will live in the higher plane of life and not permit appetite and passion to overpower your better judgment, success, wealth and happiness will great you at every turn.

Continued on page 122, also page 19.

May and July are the most favorable months for Taurus people and Friday the day to be preferred.

VIRGO.

(August 22 to September 23.)

People born under this sign, as a rule are marked by several very distinct characteristics and tendencies.

Perhaps the most prominent of these are their orderly and methodical tastes and habits. They are naturally neat, precise, accurate and discriminating, and this natural tendency is manifested in various phases of their character.

These people are usually well formed, of average height or a trifle above, with strong, intellectual, full faces, pleasing voices and agreeable manners.

They are well balanced as a general thing, and not likely to go to extremes in anything. The safe middle ground between extremes seems best to them.

Behind almost every distinguishing feature of the Virgo character it is possible to discover the two things that are must essential to their peace and comfort — Order and Harmony.

There is no method without order and the harmonious relation of all parts to the whole; and method is one of the things Virgo insists upon.

Discord and disorder cause them acute distress, and they are so sensitive to it that they discover its presence almost instantly and at once seek the cause of it or the conditions that give rise to it.

When they discover the cause or the conditions they are not content until they have at least made an effort to correct it. If it exists in affairs outside their own province, they rarely hesitate to bring it to the attention of those in whose control the matter may be, hoping it will be rectified.

Their minds, it will be seen, are very analytical and discriminating and wherever such minds aided by keen eyes are needed, Virgo people are successful.

They make the best proof readers in the world,

75

seeming able to locate the errors in a whole page at a single glance. This is one manifestation of the love of order, since an error in print is, of course, caused by the misplacing of a letter or word or line.

Their desire to have all things about them, or that they encounter, brought into harmony, leads them to take great interest in the social and love affairs of their friends and acquaintances. Their self-assumed knowledge of what is fitting and proper makes them fond of arranging matrimonial alliances among people they know; but they are equally fond of breaking off such matches as seem to them inharmonious and unsuitable.

Virgo people love music, which is the embodiment of order and harmony, and have exceptional taste in selection of color combinations. All things really beautiful appeal to them, although their inveterate habit of analysis and criticism frequently leads them to discover imaginary discrepancies, which destroy for them the real beauty of the object.

They may become very successful in editorial work, especially where they may be called upon to feel or reflect public sentiment. As book reviewers their powers of analysis and criticism are likely to make them very successful. Unless they have been awakened to the true light, however, they are apt to be severe and unkind, lacking patience with the efforts of others which do not measure up to their own self established standard.

As lawyers, writers, public speakers, musicians, architects, designers and chemists, they are qualified to achieve much distinction and honor, and it is a fact that many eminent members of the professions named have been born under Virgo.

It should be noted that the faculty of close analysis and careful presentation are essential to success in all lines, and this fact furnishes the reason for expecting Virgo people to succeed in them.

In chemistry, particularly, these people are invariably and unusually successful, their nature being especially adapted for the work. The study of physiology is peculiarly agreeable to them, also, since it is in effect the analysis of the human composition.

Virgo people are very much given to the use of medicines and remedial drugs in the effort to drive away a host of imagined ailments. It seems that their sense of order is disturbed by fancied illness or pain, and their physiological instinct advises them that some drug or medicine will restore harmony and banish the trouble. So they are nearly always going to or coming from the doctor's office, although when their knowledge of physiology is fairly advanced they often feel competent to prescribe for themselves.

Virgo people are possessed of great curiosity, which while in no sense mischievous or malicious, often gets them into ill favor. They can scarcely help taking a lively interest in the affairs of others, and are extremely fond of using their powers of observation, analysis and discrimination in ferreting out things which arouse their curiosity and thirst for information.

When thus engaged no detail is too small, no course too cunning to escape them, and every resource of their nature — diplomacy, daring, intrigue, shrewdness — is brought to bear until the problem is solved.

They have peculiar and ingenious ways of extracting information from their friends, without these latter being aware that they are giving it until it is too late and the Virgo person has learned all he wished.

They are sometimes careless of such of their friends' secrets as may come into their possession, but it is only necessary to caution them and they guard such secrets as religiously as they do their own. Their own confidence once lost is very hard to regain.

These people possess very elastic natures, and recover quickly from reverses or disappointments. There are not many of this sign who are poor in this world's goods, and it is a difficult matter to get them down, or, when they are down, to keep them there.

Even if untoward circumstances should overcome them, no matter how low they may appear to have fallen, the observant eye will not fail to discover that they still retain much of their physical and mental power.

While professional or public employment seems most attractive to Virgo people, many successful merchants and business men are found in this sign. They are quick to perceive the advantages of a business deal and do not allow many opportunities to escape them.

They have epicurean tastes, and try to get all they can out of life. While they naturally aspire to the best things, they are sometimes easily discouraged in the pursuit of them. The Virgo nature is generous and solicitous for the welfare of others.

These people are great readers, their minds retaining much of the substance of what they read, and they are able to reproduce in original form the wisdom garnered from outside sources. In this use or adaptation of borrowed thought they are very clever.

The men of this sign are fond of learning.

The women are fond of finery, dress, society and display, and will go to great lengths to gratify their desires in these particulars. They are the leaders of fashions if their circumstances permit.

Both men and women in this sign are what is termed "good dressers," their costumes being noteworthy for harmonious effects, and strikingly neat and tasteful.

This sign is the only one of the twelve which indicates absolute freedom from disease. The Virgo person needs no medicine, and should take none. Notwithstanding this demonstrated fact, they are the most inveterate medicine-takers on earth. Nature is their physician, if they but knew it. When fatigue overcomes them, or a fancied illness attacks them, an hour spent in the peaceful scenes where nature reigns among the trees and fields, "far from the haunts of men," will restore to the Virgo person its wonted elasticity and vigor. "Throw physic to the dogs," might well have been written expressly for people of this sign.

Strife, discord, disorder and inharmony are peculiarly distressing to these people, and family quarrels and bickerings especially cause them acute suffering. They are very susceptible to pain, also, and their skins are sensitive to a high degree.

These people should never partake of a meal when there is discord or anger present in themselves or their associates. This however, will apply to people of all signs.

Virgo people have an extremely strong love nature, which is, however, generally under thorough control. The women are very steadfast in their loves, and make loyal and faithful wives.

Independence seems to be a prerogative of the Virgo nature, and they prefer to live their lives in their own way. Though misfortune may overtake them, they are soon up and trying again, and usually their fate leads them to brighter futures.

There are a number of serious faults inseparable from this sign, none of which, however, are beyond hope of complete cure. It is a peculiarity of these people that they will admit an endless number of faults that they do not possess, but cannot be brought to acknowledge those that actually do afflict them.

Their principal fault is their desire to interfere with the affairs of others and to insist on other people ordering their lives and conducting their affairs along lines laid down by these self-appointed dictators.

Closely allied with this disposition is their tendency to wholesale fault finding and sharp criticism. These are very unpopular attributes, and Virgo people should learn that the most successful, congenial and popular people are those who mind their own business.

Virgo people also have a weakness for wealth and position, and many snobs, imitators and toadies disgrace this sign. False pride and unseemly ambition, too, often bring these people into disfavor. Such people have a great fondness for appearing prosperous and influential, and frequently allow themselves to become deeply involved in hopeless debt in their efforts to maintain false positions.

As previously mentioned, Virgo people are imbued with an almost unconquerable inclination to imagine that they are the victims of diseases and ailments, when the truth is they are disturbed mentally by their unfortunate habits of fault-finding and criticism. They worry over the shortcomings of others until their minds react on their bodies, and they imagine they are ill. What they really require is to get rid of their unpleasant, unprofitable habits, and to get as near to nature as they can, as often as possible.

The natural impulses of this nature is materialistic. Their deductions and conclusions are usually drawn from the material point of view. Once they cross the threshold of the spiritual domain they make rapid progress, and soon comprehend the principles of soul and spirit, becoming true teachers of the highest philosophy of human life and their immortality of the soul.

Those born in this sign who are not held in subjection by their lower natures are destined to long and useful lives, and they resist the advance of age wonderfully. Frequently at sixty they appear scarcely older than they did at thirty. Those who yield to their appetites, and dose themselves with drugs and so-called medicines, do not fare so well. It is true, nevertheless that nearly all Virgo people retain their youth and vigor to a remarkable degree.

These people are capable of great accomplishments, and of blessing humanity to an incalculable extent. They must bring themselves to realize that there is nothing absolutely perfect in this world, and that they must not expect to find perfection lying close about them.

Truth, virtue and genuine goodness and nobility of character are the things they should strive for in themselves and admire in others, rather than the superficialities, the pomp, pretense and outward show that sometimes attract by their glitter.

The perfect order and surpassing harmony that pervade the universe should impress the Virgo mind, inspiring it to absorb the beautiful lesson here to be learned, and drawing it upward to the higher life of the spirit.

Harmony, congeniality and happiness in marriage attend the union of Virgo people with those of their own sign, but it is important that there should not be great disparity between the social and intellectual attainments of the contracting parties. In Sagittarius (Nov. 22 to Dec. 21) and Libra (Sept. 23 to Oct. 23), also, Virgo people find agreeable and pleasant companionship.

In the rearing of children born in this sign, the inherent tendencies of their nature should be carefully considered. Care should be taken that they do not overhear discussion, gossip or comment on the evils of life and the faults of others. The good and true things of life should be pointed out to them, and they should be encouraged to believe that there is some good in all things. They should be prevented, if possible, from acquiring the habit of forming unkind or unjust opinions of people.

They are students by nature, and should be provided with good reading matter and thrown into the companionship of pure-minded and light-hearted people.

Pure food, pure air, kindness, with early habits of personal cleanliness and neatness, are what these little ones require.

February and November are the most fortunate months for Virgo people and Wednesday their best day.

Virgo people have at their command all the good and powerful planetary forces of the universe, and if they have the will to do so can grasp these wonderful influences and wield them to their immense and eternal advantage. If they will look for the good in the world they will find it in vast amount, and their lives will be fruitful and happy and blessed thereby. With your discriminating nature you would gain much valuable knowledge from one of the Special Horoscopes. See page 19.

6

CAPRICORN.

(December 21 to January 20.)

In appearance the people born in the sign of Capricorn are rather below the average height, and usually have dark complexions and hair, with very beautiful and expressive eyes, and usually wear glasses.

This being the head sign, the intellectual side of the nature is apt to be emphasized. These people are thinkers, reasoners, and philosophers, and aspire to the leadership or headship of whatever enterprise, association or undertaking they may be connected with.

Capricorn people are naturally inclined to study and research and devote much attention to mental culture.

When fairly educated they have a consuming desire for further learning and knowledge, and cannot rest contentedly until they have acquired the highest intellectual development within their power.

Most of these people become thoroughly conversant with natural laws, and are very helpful in the business of this strange old world. The rest of us would miss them very greatly if they were all removed.

With education and cultivation they are broadminded, liberal and tolerant, and are capable of accomplishing the great things of the world.

They throw themselves with much enthusiasm and energy into great projects and enterprises which promise material returns proportionate to their magnitude, and the superior mentality of the Capricorn nature, its fixity of purpose and contagious activity, usually bring these huge undertakings to successful completion.

These people have positively executive ability in large degree, and being determined in their tendencies they naturally aspire to be recognized as the head or leading spirit in every activity in which they engage.

If this leadership is denied or impossible of achievement, they are more than likely to lose interest in the matter.

They feel instinctively their sense of fitness for position or rank above the common level; they feel that wealth and power should be theirs in bountiful measure.

It is unfortunate if they chance to be born to poverty, for failing to receive or achieve those things to which they believe themselves entitled, and not being inspired to effort by results that might seem sufficient to others, they permit themselves to sink to the lowest depths of despondency.

Frequently after having met with reverses of fortune these people positively refuse to adapt themselves to changed conditions, but spend recklessly until their resources are completely exhausted.

They are proud, independent and high minded, and indisposed to labor with their own hands, unless it may be, possibly, to accomplish some task that will lead to higher opportunities.

They are better contented and more successful, usually when engaged in business for themselves than when employed in the service of others.

They are extremely industrious, but are likely to undertake too many different things at the same time.

As entertainers the Capricorn people have few equals, the diversion they provide being of an intellectual order. Their fund of amusing anecdotes and appropriate stories is always ample, and they know how and when to introduce them into the conversation.

As might be expected, some very eloquent public speakers, profound philosophers, eminent actors and men of deep learning have come from the sign of Capricorn. Clay Clement, Sir Isaac Newton, Daniel Webster, and Wm. E. Gladstone are among those whose birth was in this sign.

It is noteworthy, also, that the very best teachers come from Capricorn. They are naturally patient, careful of details, and usually gentle and kind. Students always make rapid progress under them, study-ing hard and striving to advance because of their de-sire to show their affection and admiration for their instructor.

No matter what pursuit they may undertake, Capri-corn people go about attaining excellence therein with a calm, quiet determination that is well nigh irresistible. So cautious is their advance that they may seem to be making not the slightest progress; but in the end they will usually be found to have reached the goal for which they started.

When these people become aware of the true ideals in life, and strive to attain them, they frequently be-come tireless, enthusiastic and effective workers in the cause of religion, being most valuable members of the church of their choice.

Flattery, even the most subtle and skillful, is wasted on people of this sign, and they not only scorn but are apt to resent it. They are highly magnetic, and people are attracted to them without effort on their part.

They do not act on impulse, nor are they very de-monstrative, being generally cool-headed and deliberate, yet they know their real friends, appreciate their friendship, and are never at a loss to distinguish be-tween empty flattery and sincere commendation.

The women of this sign are extremely sensible, and even better managers than the men. In money mat-ters they are discreet and prudent, and are especially qualified to arrange and manage their homes. They are well fitted for the duties of housekeepers in hotels or public institutions where numerous servants are em-ployed.

These women prefer power to love, pretty dresses to pretty speeches, and high social standing above all else. They stand coldly aloof in their own conscious intellectual superiority, silently reminding others of their defects and shortcomings. In their presence the ordinary mortal cannot long remain unaware of his uncouthness of manner, his inelegant diction and his deficiency of booklore.

The desire of the Capricorn nature to maintain prosperous appearances and to keep pace with fashionable aristocracy frequently causes them much embarrassment and distress.

They are fond of travel and are veritable globetrotters if their means permit.

They love harmony and beauty, and musical talent is sometimes given them in abundance. These traits should be cultivated, especially that for music, as music is extremely beneficial to the Capricorn nature. The sign has produced a number of very famous composers and performers.

These people are often very successful in business affairs. They deserve to succeed, being conservative, secretive, cautious in money matters, natural planners and providers, and disposed to mind their own business very strictly.

It sometimes occurs that Capricorn people are eccentric and incautious in their charities and investments. This depends on their mood. They are either highly cheerful optimists or deeply gloomy pessimists. They see the world through glasses tinted either with the rosy glow of hope or with the sombre blue or drab of despair. And their temporary frame of mind imparts itself to their dealings with others.

Education and culture are essential to proper development of the Capricorn nature, but must be supplemented by strong desire and resolve to live in the higher atmosphere of the spirit, if all possible good may follow.

The natural faults of this sign are selfishness, lack of concentration, distrust of self, pride and vanity. When these faults are analyzed it will be seen that they arise mainly from too constant mental dwelling on the material needs and desires, and from considerable self-love.

These people seem to imagine their worries and anxieties to be not only of the most importance, but also that they are of great interest to others. Then they are led to indiscretions of speech as to quantity and manner, which cause them considerable trouble.

Those who make careful and critical study of themselves, thus discovering their weak points, and who then set diligently to work to overcome those weaknesses, are the people of this sign who achieve success and honor.

When the higher nature dominates the organism, checking and subduing the lower animal tendencies, the faults and defects of character melt away as mists beneath the morning sun.

Then they possess all that is truly worth having. They become illumined with spiritual light, and their power for good has no bounds. It may require severe and prolonged effort to attain this blissful state, but the reward is more than ample, for there can be no happier or more truly prosperous people on earth than the Capricorn born who have come into their heritage.

In contracting marriages, people of this sign should seek alliances with those from Taurus (April 19 to May 22) if they wish vigorous offspring. Marriage with Libra (Sept. 23 to Oct. 23) or Virgo (Aug. 22 to Sept. 23) are also usually harmonious and congenial.

Children born under Capricorn are peculiarly constituted, and require peculiarly careful training and government. They very readily reflect their surrounding conditions, and for that reason should not be permitted to associate with any but refined and good mannered companions. If not controlled, these little folks will become haughty, arrogant and troublesome, yet parents should never permit themselves to display any temper in their management of the children. They may be trained only by intense love and tenderness combined with unyielding firmness.

Simple tastes should be inculcated early in life, in dress, in habits and in eating especially, and they should learn that outward display is usually low and vulgar.

Capricorn people of all ages and both sexes are especially rich in the planetary influences and solar fluids which perpetually surround. These influences, rightly understood and employed, are beneficial in the highest degree. To achieve success, it is only necessary for the Capricorn person to make choice of some congenial occupation, profession, business or art, concentrate their energy and purpose on that pursuit, and march straight ahead to victory, aided by the mysterious forces that are at their command.

The diseases in this sign are indigestion and melancholia, or the blues. These are brought on by overwork, worry and too great anxiety to succeed. To have perfect health, these people must banish worry and anxiety and be confident that all things are working together for their good. When they do this they enjoy splendid health and live long and useful lives.

You place your main dependence upon your head. The power to plan, organize and think, using the head instead of the hands, in fact nature never intended you to work with your hands and you even dislike laborious or dirty work that must be performed with the hands, while with the head you throw your entire mental force into the execution of any task at hand. Your greatest achievement and success lies in planning, organizing, systematizing and with your broad active brain full of speculative desire and meditations you are capable of combatting with the gigantic problems of life where deep thought is required, bringing things down to a system in such places. You are best satisfied, providing there is promise of suitable return to warrant and justify the efforts, yet you would lose personal interest in a small or unimportant task.

You dislike detail work, thinking your time worthy of a better cause. You have a great desire for wealth and to live in luxury and ease with aspirations to be above the level of the masses, you will recall that it is most difficult for you to economize in the small matters of life. With your natural power of economy and system you are capable of making ends meet. We are all put here in the world for a purpose and your place is to be a figure-head in the business world and to work your way to the head of some great corporation or commercial enterprise, in this way you will be going with the tide as you have a natural desire for power.

Children born under this sign are most apt to become head-strong, self-willed, with a desire to rule those about them.

The elders are sure to say that the child has such old ways, in reality they are old when young and young when old. They are old-fashioned little folks with old heads on young shoulders.

From the 19th to the 21st year is most likely to prove unfortunate. At the 25th year there will be a change brought about in your life for either, better or worse, as this is a turning point. You may expect at least two or three ups and downs between your 30th and 42nd year, and after these dates life will become much brighter as the years pass.

Your Horoscope shows many bright opportunities, and while your tastes are shown to be luxurious, it is quite difficult for you to economize in small matters. You are a born leader in the business world and highly capable of assuming leadership, responsibility and a natural instigator of stupendous undertakings.

Your success and rise in the world will come about in a mysterious way, and unexpected too. There is much to be said about your eventful life, but space will not permit in this wonderful book, though enough has been said to convince you of the real worth of the author and his valuable book on Astrology.

A Special Horoscope would no doubt become of priceless value to you throughout your life. There are many lines therein, that would be worth many times the cost of the work. See page 19.

CANCER.

(June 21 to July 22.)

This is a fickle and doubtful sign, extremely hard to understand, and seeming to partake of the change-ability of its governing planet, the moon.

In many directions they are gifted and talented almost to the point of genius and like many geniuses they are alluring, unstable, never quite definable and may be improvident, living from hand to mouth.

They are among the most attractive people one ever meets, in personal appearance. They are usually of medium stature, rather inclined to full chest and bust development, with round, pleasing faces, delicate features, light or grayish eyes and tawny or pale complexions. Their constitutions are not likely to be strong.

The lower or undeveloped types of Cancer people present an almost incomprehensible array of contradictory emotions and desires, and these people are very often the greatest puzzles to their friends and associates clear to the end of the chapter.

Perhaps their most marked characteristic is their changefulness and uncertainty. One never knows what to expect from them. They make apparently firm decisions, decide upon a course of action, or fix upon an object to be accomplished, and then in a very brief time all these are cast aside and new ones, or none at all, are substituted. Or they may reverse themselves completely and set out on a course directly opposite to that originally intended.

The mental attitude of these people is powerfully affected by the alternation of day and night, rain and sunshine. Their whole personality and all their ideas frequently undergo complete change as the day draws to its close and darkness covers the earth.

What was to them the veriest truth in the glare of

artificial light may become utter fallacy in the searching scrutiny of the sunshine.

This tendency to change frequently impels them to give up one occupation and embark in another, with scarcely any reason except their overwhelming restlessness. They also take many long trips in search of new and untried scenes and experiences, but seldom reach the desired success.

Cancer people also display this same inexplicable mutability of nature in their relations with friends and associates. They sometimes discard old and pleasant friendships without either warning or reason, at a moment's notice, and are fully capable of feeling and showing bitter enmity to those who were formerly their closest and best friends.

The friendships thus sacrificed are rarely if ever renewed.

Cancer people are very jealous, and demand from others the constancy they themselves do not possess.

Fickleness and inconstancy are strongly emphasized in both men and women of this sign who are living on the lower plane, and should they marry much unhappiness is unavoidable. The women, however, are less constant than the men, and will go to almost any extreme, and make any sacrifice, to gratify their pronounced fondness for fine wearing apparel, jewels, display and admiration.

They demand homage and flattery on all occasions, and if it is not granted in full measure they make themselves and all about them decidedly uncomfortable.

Unless they are constantly humored and petted, they recall past attentions and devotion with gloomy persistency, comparing those welcome evidences of affection with the present lack of them, and enumerating a long list of petty ailments and imaginary slights calculated to melt the hardest heart.

It must be said that the men of this sign are much more agreeable than their sisters. They display less affection and will listen more patiently to reason.

They are of a saving disposition in money matters and have a deep dread of poverty.

Cancer born people are extremely sensitive, but theirs is the sensitiveness of wounded pride rather than that of affection misunderstood or misplaced. They are vain and imperious rather than loving, and would not exchange one iota of their power for all the love in the world.

This sensitiveness extends to all the affairs of their lives, and subjects them to easy and frequent discouragement. They resent the most kindly meant criticism, construing it as a reflection upon themselves, and become irritable, moody and melancholy as a result.

A word or even a look which they imagine is unfavorable is often sufficient to discourage them in whatever project they may be engaged and to lead them to entirely abandon even great undertakings.

People of this sign are particularly sensitive in affairs of the finer feelings or of the heart, and are greatly dejected by a fancied slight from one for whom they care.

This sensitiveness is the key to the nature of these people and by skillfully playing upon this delicately attuned chord unworthy and designing persons are often able to capture and vanquish the citadel of their hearts and affections.

They are neither broad minded nor open to conviction. Argument is useless with them. Logic and reason are of no avail. They can be stubborn to an unbelievable extent.

Turning from these unlovely manifestations of the sway of evil over the Cancer nature, it is a pleasure to record that they are exceedingly kind and gentle to those for whom they care, in seasons of illness and trouble.

Their hearts are quickly and deeply touched by suffering, and for those who are crippled or afflicted they display the utmost tenderness, consideration and sympathy.

This is particularly true of the women of this sign, who are also the home makers of earth. Like the men, they have an inborn craving to travel — to visit new scenes; but once this is overcome or satisfied they are very domestic and become almost perfect wives and mothers.

These women also have an inclination to engage in literary pursuits.

Cancer people are greatly devoted to their families and are fearless in guarding the rights and lives of those they love.

Cancer people frequently live in constant dread of a visit from burglars, and conceal their valuables in many strange places, although the old-fashioned stocking is a favorite safe deposit vault with them.

They have a natural tendency toward the beautiful and artistic in all things, and as a result some highly talented musicians, artists and professional people come out of this sign.

They have mechanical ability, also, and the men are likely to be able to suggest and work out many improvements in time and labor-saving machinery.

Occasionally a gifted and powerful public speaker comes from Cancer, and some of the greatest scholars and students, as well as some of the richest people in the world, have been born under it.

The men are well adapted to succeed in manufacturing and active trades, and in ordinary mercantile business.

Educated Cancer people are highly progressive, and their anxiety to better the condition of mankind prompts them to great and beneficent works of public charity and philanthropy.

These people aspire to be at the head of all undertakings with which they are identified, and cannot achieve any marked degree of usefulness or success in subordinate positions.

They are confirmed globe-trotters and are likely to wander over a large part of the earth before they settle down.

When not developed these people are prone to talk of themselves and their wonderful accomplishments and the marvels they have witnessed, and if not checked this tendency becomes a most disagreeable habit, earning for its possessor a reputation for boasting and exaggeration.

So much of this chapter has been given to detailing the unfavorable points of the Cancer nature that it is unnecessary to recapitulate them under the grouping of "faults."

It must not be understood, however, that their characters are all bad. On the contrary they possess many lovable and commendable traits, and they require only to learn and practice the true method of life to develop into splendid people.

They are naturally endowed with strength of purpose, and when they form an honest intention to overcome their faults, and persist in this intention with all their might, they are most successful.

Education and mental cultivation are of incalculable value to these Cancer people. Planetary and solar influences are very favorable to them in an awakened state, but very unfavorable to those who are unenlightened.

At heart all Cancer people are good and desirous of doing right by themselves and their fellow creatures, and they should strive honestly and persistently to develop and encourage these inner promptings until they dominate their lower natures entirely.

Their happiness, usefulness and progress depend altogether upon their own efforts. The evils in the Cancer nature are among the easiest to overcome, and the reward of the victory is so grand and complete and delightful that no one of this sign should be content with any other plane of life than the highest.

Persons born under this sign should under no circumstance associate with or be under the care of persons that are in the least degree repulsive to them, and this applies to old and young.

Failure to guard against this has frequently caused

the death of persons of this sign, from cancerous or tumorous affections.

It is one of the misfortunes of these people that persons whose influence is very disagreeable will often insist upon forcing themselves on the Cancer people, and it is extremely difficult to get rid of them. Such persons absorb and feed upon the vitality of the Cancer-born, depleting it to the danger point.

Cancer-born people will find Pisces people (Feb. 19 to March 21) noble and unselfish, but those from Scorpio (Oct. 23 to Nov. 22) will prove the most constant and best in the end.

Marriage to those born in this sign is a most hazardous step, and they should defer it until well along in life. They should never marry until they feel that they have complete control over the fickleness and inconstancy that beset them.

Children born in this sign are so organized that their rearing and training require the highest degree of judgment and discrimination.

They are exceedingly difficult to manage, but when thoroughly understood and treated kindly and lovingly they become very tractable and gentle.

They should be guarded, when young, from contemplation of the more sombre aspects of life, and should never be left long in the presence of illness or suffering, or allowed to attend funerals.

They are fond of fancy dresses and it is well to gratify this taste within reasonable bounds. Overdressing, however, may prove a calamity, especially in the case of Cancer girls.

These children should sleep alone, and must not be kissed and caressed by strangers. Their diet should be simple, plain and nourishing.

The fundamental truths of life should be imparted to them as early as these things can be comprehended, and open frankness should take the place of false modesty and prudishness in dealing with Cancer children. Abundance of rest and sleep are essential to their well being.

You have had some trying experiences in your past life which has been a most eventful one. The writer wishes to state that the only true way that you can ever hope to realize the great possibilities that await you is through determination and perseverance. Never to release or relax — but ever on until your efforts have been crowned with success.

Nature has gifted you with more than the usual amount of power to organize and execute the great problems of the world.

Among the names of Cancer people, are enrolled not only the richest, but as well the greatest in all history, names that are known to the four corners of the earth — mostly from the farms or the district school, such as John Wanamaker, John D. Rockefeller, Stuyvesant Fish, Dr. Cyrenius Wakefield, Robert Ball and Kelvin; Astronomers, Rubens, Painter; George Eastman, inventor of the Kodak; George M. Cohen, and the great phenomenon, Miss Helen Keller, who shall forever live in the hearts of the English speaking people and with much due credit to her teacher.

With those of this sign after the start is once made on the road to success the progress then becomes most rapid, you can achieve the best and highest things or be an utter failure, it lies with yourself for you to decide as to what extreme you shall go.

Your tastes are inclined to be luxurious. You display remarkable skill with the use of your hands and being positively shrewd in all business matters.

Occupation — Inventor, Promoter, Lawyer, Physician, Merchant and Salesman.

You will likely cover a great portion of the globe if circumstances will permit as there is ever a fondness for travel and objects to amuse.

February and September are the most favorable months for Cancer people, and Monday the day to be preferred.

Every seven years there will be a change brought about in your life. The purpose of a Complete Horoscope is to explain these details.

SCORPIO.

(October 23 to November 22.)

"Be brave, be true in all you do;
Make sure you're right, then force the fight,
Holding honor high,
Being fully determined to win or die."

Persons born under this sign are usually of robust physical nature, with a reserved and undemonstrative dignity of appearance. They incline to corpulency in middle life, and are nearly always of a brunette type, with broad and open countenances.

The sign of their birth indicates a self-centered although somewhat restless nature, in which great determination and will power are marked characteristics. They seem destined to encounter strange vicissitudes of fortune, resulting from their vaulting ambition and their restless energy.

These natures are related to the mysterious powers of the ocean, and are possessed of marvelous vitality through the operation of vibratory forces, electromagnetic currents and solar fluids, all of which constantly influence their existence. These influences frequently are so pronounced in persons of this sign that they are endowed with wonderful powers of healing and soothing, through which they are enabled to be of immense benefit and comfort to those who are closely connected with them.

Scorpio people are irresistibly attracted by enterprises and projects characterized by novelty, daring and uncertainty, and their pertinacity, grit and determination, impel them to herculean achievements in overcoming obstacles and surmounting difficulties. The more difficult and daring the project, and the more overwhelming its magnitude, the greater fascination it possesses for them, and the greater the probability of their success. Yet they are not content with their own accomplishments, but each victory won, only spurs them to further efforts in other fields, and they seem to rejoice more in the struggle and stress of doing than in the sense of completion of a task. They are often successful in establishing a business or putting an enterprise in operation, in the face of great obstacles and difficulties, but when the hardest of the work is done they look around for other fields to conquer.

Their self control is admirable, and manifests itself not only in their reserve in speaking, but in the firmness, sureness and deftness of their hands with which is combined keen powers of observation and rare poise and judgment.

These traits fit them to become skilled craftsmen, excellent designers, and eminent surgeons. In the latter calling, their utter lack of useless sentiment, their unerring judgment and their cool and calm self-possession, are likely to carry them to the very front rank of their profession.

This calmness, determination and stern practicality sometimes gives rise to the charge that Scorpio people are without sympathy, hard and unfeeling, but as a matter of fact they are among the kindest hearted people in the world. Their sympathy, instead of venting itself in ineffectual words, takes the much better form of clear headed, helpful actions and deeds that bring comfort and relief to the distressed.

Sometimes men of this sign become very powerful and magnetic orators and preachers, possessing the true genius of eloquence. When developed by education and culture, they acquire great tact and taste in the use of language, and their words exert much force and influence upon their hearers.

Sometimes this facility of language in this sign finds expression in literature, and their brilliant imaginations, continually striking out into untried paths and unknown fields, win for them much success in short story writing.

7

By the cultivation of the attributes with which they are endowed from the hour of their birth they are equipped to rise to almost any heights. Their dignified bearing, their calm and sensible speech, and their self-assurance, gain for them the confidence and esteem of others, and their persistency carries them as far as they wish to go.

These people usually display very original and artistic tastes, and are exceedingly fond of luxurious surroundings, both at home and in places of business. As a rule they are successful in accumulating wealth, and live very comfortably. They have excellent taste in dress as in all things else, but are more impressed by actual worth than by mere lavish display.

Outdoor sports appeal very strongly to them, and much of their leisure time is given to such pastimes. The ocean, or any body of water which has the charm of majesty, power, beauty or picturesqueness, possesses great attraction for them, and they are fond of travel and adventure on water, as well as of the beauty of lake or river scenery.

Usually polite, considerate and of pleasant demeanor, they can be blunt even to cruelty when engrossed by serious affairs.

Many of the people born in this sign, living on the lower or animal plane, have never been awakened to realize the limitless possibilities that are theirs. When awakened and spiritualized they are helpful, kind, gentle, considerate and benevolent; but when engrossed in money making or some one purpose they can be and often are very selfish and mean. They are always busy, and having no time to meddle with others' affairs, they nearly always succeed in their own.

Scorpio people are very likely to be confirmed procrastinators. While it is true that their magnificent powers usually enable them to carry through their undertakings, it is also true that they delay and put off matters on the slightest pretext or on no pretext whatever. This characteristic is the cause of much concern to their associates and those with whom they have dealings, and should be easily overcome if the Scorpio person will make up his mind to the task.

Their self-esteem and approbativeness are ordinarily very highly developed, and occasionally they are quite susceptible to flattery.

Those of this sign who live on the animal or material plane have a number of very serious faults or bad tendencies. Until these are corrected they cannot hope to attain the highest degree of happiness or prosperity. We point out these weaknesses and infirmities, and urge upon Scorpio readers the necessity of giving them serious and thoughtful attention. Astrology is an exact science which will greatly benefit and assist those who earnestly aspire to make the most of their lives. Almost any teaching or advice is wasted on the foolish.

Many Scorpio people have been lost and destroyed through anger, jealousy and passion. The intense desire for praise and flattery is another weakness of the lower types of this sign.

Scorpio women are prone to cause their husbands much annoyance and distress if the husband neglects the constant practice of flattery, praise and admiration of the wife.

Sometimes the demon of jealousy takes possession of men of this sign, and the intensity of their natures drives them to the verge of murderous frenzy. Those who have not learned the higher law of love are eccentric and unreasonable in their affections. Jealousy frequently attacks the women of this sign, too, commonly without any justification; and these women who have not acquired self-control are the worst naggers in the world, making themselves and all about them miserable and wretched.

Among the unawakened of this sign, the lower instincts — lust, slothfulness, greed, vulgarity, cruelty and selfishness — are likely to assume full sway; and the very intensity of their natures, with its persistency, imagination, courage and self-assertiveness, makes them as powerful for evil, against themselves and against others, as they would be for good were their higher natures awakened.

Their selfishness leads them to make all possible use of their friends, toward whom they assume the most pleasing attitude so long as anything is to be gained thereby; but as soon as their friends cease to be useful, or the desired object is attained through them, they are tossed aside as lightly as one discards a worn-out glove; yet should circumstances again make these discarded ones desirable for any reason, the Scorpio does not hesitate to seek to renew friendly relations, and possessing so magnetic a personality, they usually succeed in winning back their shabbily-treated friends and in securing their forgiveness and their confidence.

Their fondness for high living and the unbridled sway of their baser passions render these people particularly liable to attacks of gout, rheumatism, heart trouble, lumbago and weakness of the back.

Being so susceptible to flattery, they fail to realize that one true friend is worth any army of flatterers, yet this truth is one of the most important for them to learn.

These people can accomplish any ambition, however lofty; they can make for themselves high stations among the nobility of mankind, and to do this they need only overcome their faults and weaknesses. Each of them should set apart a certain time each day for self-communion and self-examination. It is very difficult for them to acknowledge their faults, even to themselves; but the exercise of their tremendous will power will enable them mercilessly to apply the probe of self-examination and to overcome the weaknesses and failings that must otherwise drag them lower and lower.

Once their feet are placed by their own efforts and struggles, on the higher moral plane, their enlightened mentality will show them the darkness from which they have emerged and the glory and beauty of the path they may tread if they will.

Scorpio people find their most congenial companions among those born under Pisces (Feb. 19 to March 21). Good, staunch friends are to be found, also, in Libra (Sept. 23 to Oct. 23) and Virgo (Aug. 22 to Sept. 23).

In marriage, Scorpio and Virgo people make happy and prosperous mates, the offspring being vigorous physically and brilliant mentally. Libra and Scorpio, or Scorpio and Pisces, do not promise so well in the marriage relation. It must be borne in mind that the happiest marriages may be expected only where the contracting parties are on an equal footing socially and intellectually.

Occupations — Surgery, Chemistry, Architect, House and Floral Decorator, displaying remarkable skill with the use of the hands.

In this sign the sexual nature is unusually strong and until you have stopped dissipating your life's energies you can never hope to achieve success in any calling. You could neither plan methodically or think clearly, and your undertakings will surely meet with failure in the end if you permit base animal passion to predominate and rob you of the excellent judgment you would otherwise possess.

Children born under this sign are usually quite domineering, and this tendency should be corrected as early as possible. They must be quietly reared and taught to amuse and entertain themselves, early in life. When they reach the age of understanding, they should be led by gentle and loving, though firm hands, into paths of right and truth. They should be given every attainable educational advantage since they have within them the highest possibilities for acquiring knowledge and for applying it to the greatest good.

January and July are the more fortunate months with preference given to Tuesday. See page 118.

PISCES.

(February 19 to March 21.)

Those who enter the arena of life while this sign
is in the ascendant are usually of pleasing appearance,
with full faces, dreamy, peaceful eyes and a generally
retiring demeanor. They are not inclined to erect car-
riage, being frequently rather stoop shouldered.

These people do not belie their personal appearance.
They are thoughtful and peaceful by nature and they
seem to have become bowed down under the weight
of the cares of the world which they take voluntarily
upon themselves.

Deep and most kindly sympathy for the afflicted,
distressed and suffering among their fellowmen is very
characteristic of this sign.

They have an intense desire to acquire knowledge of
all kinds, preferring, however, to acquaint themselves
with scientific and philosophical subjects. History and
tales of travel also attract them, but they own to a
broad taste, and gather information and learning from
all available sources.

With all this, however, they are extremely modest
and are never guilty of the bad taste of parading their
knowledge or making a display of their learning.

Their modesty, which so often stands in the way of
their best interests, is augmented by a lack of confidence in themselves, no matter how great their abilities and attainments.

The acquisitiveness and retentiveness of the Pisces
mind, where knowledge and information is involved,
make them sometimes veritable "walking encyclope-
dies," yet even in such cases they betray a woeful lack
of self-confidence.

They may devote much thought and study to a
subject, and acquire the fullest knowledge of it from
every possible source, becoming satisfied in their own

minds that they have arrived at the truth concerning it — and still hesitate to present their views to the public.

The more honest and honorable they are the greater their hesitancy. They seem to fear that they may not be able to fulfill their promises, or that the world will expect more of them than they can fulfill.

Add to these traits a boundless generosity and absolute unselfishness, and the reason is plain why these Pisces people are so frequently found occupying stations in life far below their real deserts.

Pisces people are very sensible folks, careful, anxious and somewhat restless.

Especially are they concerned about money matters, and anxious to make such provision for the future as will assure them an independent living. They take commendable pride in the feeling that they are not indebted to any one for whatever they may possess, and that they fairly earn all they may receive. This sentiment affords them double pleasure in the enjoyment of the fruits of their labors.

They instinctively shrink from placing themselves under obligations to others, and are extremely reluctant to ask favors or accommodations for themselves.

These people are absolutely trust-worthy and honorable in all their relations with their fellowmen. With proper training they become ideal cashiers, book-keepers and accountants.

Possessing so strict a sense of honor and fidelity, and being simple-hearted and unsuspicious, Pisces people usually believe other men to be equally honest and reliable. This makes them easy victims of shrewd and unscrupulous schemers, and their disappointment at such times is very great.

People who realize the kindness and self-effacement of these people often make use of them to advance their own fortunes, and, so far from feeling resentment, the patient, liberal-souled Pisces person rejoices in the success to which he has contributed. It does not occur to him that he may have practically robbed himself of splendid opportunities by his unselfishness and lack of self-seeking; nor would it make any difference if he know such to be the case.

This whole-hearted generosity is at once one of the most lovable and the least commendable traits of the Pisces character. No man has a right to be generous before he is just; and justice demands that he shall not suffer by his openhandedness. Yet the people of this sign will often deprive themselves greatly in order to help others, and then bemoan their inability to give more.

This phase of character seems to contradict their concern as to financial matters, yet it is but an indication of their entire lack of self love. They think it would be unfair to let any one else suffer if they could prevent it, and that they themselves are of so little account they need not be considered.

This feeling will account for their anxiety for the future. Holding themselves so cheaply they imagine that others place a low valuation on them and their accomplishments and fear the time may come when they will not be able successfully to compete with others.

They have a further tendency to gloomy forebodings, and imagine countless evils where none exist. They are heavy borrowers at the bank of trouble, and cross many a bridge they never reach.

Pisces people will find a limited amount of travel very beneficial and their natural inclinations in this direction should be gratified so far as possible.

They love beauty in art and nature, and are fond of wide expanses of sea or land. Spring scenes, particularly in early morning, fill them with quiet enjoyment, although they are almost equally happy in the peaceful twilight shading softly into dusk.

Placidity and calmness are parts of the Pisces nature, and these people should cultivate these characteristics, avoiding worry and anxiety, especially in business affairs.

Some of the most noted and sucessful financiers in

the world have come out of this sign. They are attentive to details, accurate and absolutely upright — qualifications which are essential to success in finance.

Many people of this sign become musicians, artists, art critics, poets and writers. They have an unfailing instinct for the picturesque and their work in every line gives evidence of the noble, simple, humanity-loving nature which animates it.

Having once made choice of an occupation or vocation, Pisces people usually adhere to it, or to some line of activity related to it, throughout their lives. It will be seen then, that it is of the utmost importance that they should make a wise choice and enter a calling for which they are best fitted by nature.

They should choose a "field" where there are plenty of opportunities for advancement, and where their unquestionable capacity for work, their fidelity to trust, and their readiness to learn will be recognized and rewarded. In such a field their success is assured.

These people are particularly cleanminded, and have no place in their hearts for anything that savors of impurity, vulgarity or coarseness.

They are deeply religious, but become at times intolerant in the fervor of their attachment to some particular creed or church.

The women of this sign are exceedingly fond of home and its environments when they have overcome or satisfied their inborn restlessness and desire to travel. Then they become truly ideal wives and mothers, and display most excellent taste and skill in the adornment and conduct of their homes.

The most advantageous arrangement that can be made by people in this sign is to associate themselves either socially or in business life with some one who possesses more originality than themselves, because while Pisces people are capable of carrying out the plans and suggestions of other brilliantly and carefully, they do not possess the initiative to plan or invent new projects and improvements. Great mutual benefits should arise from association with Capricorn (Dec. 21

to Jan. 20), whether the connection be marital, commercial or merely friendly.

By some irony of fate, however, Pisces people almost invariably offer their devotion at the shrine of those from Libra (Sept. 23 to Oct. 23) and their affection is heartily reciprocated. Fortunately they are seldom permitted to unite with Libra, those born in Capricorn (Dec. 21 to January 20) are by far the more desirable and will endure to eternity.

Men of this sign are fitted to adorn the legal profession. Their strict sense of justice, their capacity for accumulating knowledge, and their magnetic personalities, inspiring others with a sense of their fairness and honesty, should fit them to win those cases in which they are ranged upon the side of truth and right.

The faults associated with this sign are not of a vicious nature; in fact, their untoward tendencies are practically the same as diseases, which may be removed by proper self treatment.

Fretfulness, impatience, overanxiety and worrying are the faults which cause most trouble in this sign.

It is by no means rare that Pisces people age themselves prematurely by the loss of vitality caused by their diseased imaginations. They are in constant dread of accidents and calamities of all kinds, while as a matter of fact the greater part of all their fears are groundless.

These people need the aid of a kind, firm and loving hand to lend them re-assurance and self-confidence, and to guide them to the road that leads to fame and fortune. They are naturally inclined to self-censure, but are susceptible to earnest and disinterested advice from those in whom they believe.

They must learn to press forward with confidence in themselves and in the right, overcoming obstacles and resisting temptations, and in time will surely learn that often a seeming misfortune may prove to be a great blessing instead, opening the way to their highest triumphs.

Their nervous apprehensions make them morbid,

restless, uncertain, and sometimes drive them to the extremity of self-destruction.

Carelessness in habits, in dress, and in most of life's affairs is another result of their abnormal mental condition due to excessive worry and anxiety.

Sometimes these people suddenly seize the courage of desperation, throw off the shackles of timidity and fear, and rebel violently against their lot. In such cases they lose all sense of propriety, propose and attempt the most absurd things and stoutly resist all attempts to placate them.

They are deaf to reason at such times, as well as to persuasion or advice, becoming more obstinate and stubborn the more one endeavors to bring them to their senses.

Undeveloped people of this sign frequently make themselves disagreeable by interrupting conversations without excuse, by asking silly or irrelevant questions, and by talking too freely.

These undeveloped people are not gifted with much judgment. They worry themselves sick over things they cannot help, and they impoverish themselves by giving way to their generous but misguided impulses.

All these defects in the Pisces character will yield to the influence of true wisdom. With their capacity and thirst for knowledge, these people surely can learn to be sensible. Meditation and the study of philosophy will help them greatly. They should frequently seek out some peaceful, quiet retreat, where they can commune with nature and search their beings for the causes of their distress.

Courage, confidence and perseverance — these three things are the greatest needs of the Pisces character. With these virtues developed as they can be, and backed by the truly sterling worth of those in this sign, there are no accomplishments beyond their powers, no heights to which they may not climb, no more helpful, success-ful and beneficent people in the world than they.

They have practically boundless possibilities for good, which they can attain by compelling the less worthy parts of their nature to acknowledge the supremacy of the higher; and in this task they will be aided by the powerful forces for good that radiate through them, in moments of calm receptivity, from the planets of the universe.

When their spiritual natures are developed, they are very agreeable and lovable persons, breathing purity and sweetness and spreading peace and contentment all about them.

With their faults driven out forever, the innate strength of their natures will enable them to command and achieve the highest measure of success in any walk of life.

Children born in this sign are unusually precocious and brilliant, exceedingly sensitive, and likely to early display their loving tendencies and generous impulses.

Parents and guardians should not fall into the error of believing that these traits of generosity and tendency to give away all they possess are desirable or praiseworthy in these children. Unless wisely restrained, these traits will grow to inordinate dimensions, to gratify which the children will sometimes get into the habit of taking things that do not belong to them, that they may give to others.

These loving little ones should know nothing but constant love and uniform kindness. They must be taught habits of order and neatness, and their will power judiciously strengthened. One might better break the neck of a Pisces child than attempt to break his will.

Their intuitive taste for knowledge should be wisely cultivated and directed into proper channels, and they should never be allowed to indulge in or overhear discouraging forebodings or gloomy prophecies.

To Pisces people, May and June are the most propitious months, and Saturday the favorable day.

THE CUSPS.

In astrological calculations, the first six days of the ascendancy of any particular sign, constitute what is called the "cusp" of that sign, and the influence of the sign is to a greater or less extent governed and modified by the influence of the sign immediately preceding.

Thus, those born on the "cusp" of Leo are to some degree subject to the influence of Cancer, and so through all the signs.

We shall give a brief delineation of the probable characteristics of persons born in the twelve cusps. By carefully studying the two signs involved in any particular cusp, the student of this work will be able to arrive at safe and reasonable conclusions as to the natural traits and tendencies of those born therein.

The Cusp — Aries and Taurus.

(April 19 to 25.)

Those born at this time are usually blessed with large forms and broad shoulders. They are not always robust, but have a wiry nature, — and this is true of both physical and mental qualifications.

They are strong intellectually, and of a very determined and confident mold, have unlimited faith in their own knowledge, and give advice constantly and freely to relatives and friends. Their strongly magnetic personalities make them very persuasive, so that their advice is hard to decline or resist. At the same time, these people themselves are the last of all to accept advice from others.

In fact they may be called strong headed, and are very persistent in their undertakings, frequently being utterly heedless of advisement, no matter how great the expense that may be involved, nor how deep and

109

true the knowledge of those who would tender suggestions and criticisms.

These people have excellent taste in all things, and delight in the pleasures of the table. They find much enjoyment, also, in giving evidence of their thoughtfulness of their friends, in the way of gifts, dinners, etc. For children they possess great fondness, and include them in their kindly remembrances.

If these people will only be guided by the higher inspirations, their accomplishments will be unlimited and will yield them a bounteous harvest of all the world's best gifts. Their possibilities are of the grandest and most noble, and they need only determine to possess them and they can do so.

When living on the lower plane, they frequently sink very low in sensuality, dissipation and vice, dropping eventually to the very last rung in the ladder.

The Cusp — Taurus and Gemini.

(May 20 to 26.)

To those born on this cusp, it is of the utmost importance that they shall acquire rigid and complete self-control. Possessing this, and developing the better side of their natures, these people are capable of much good to themselves and others, being highly organized and well endowed with talents of many kinds.

They are the thinkers, orators, artists and inventors, and their hands and brains work together in perfect harmony.

They display exceptionally good taste in dress, and their manners and habits are refined and pleasing.

They are successful in nearly all occupations and professions, and are always active and energetic.

Without proper early training, they frequently develop exceedingly large bodies, and are addicted to sensuousness and sometimes sensuality. The men grow large about the neck and abdomen, are loud and boisterous, careless in manners, speech, dress and reputation. The women, under such conditions, are hysterical and often chronically nervous and helpless.

These people, when living on the lower plane, carry their tendencies to extremes. They are very active and lively when in good spirits, and very indolent and morose when depressed.

If in humble circumstances they are very miserable, displaying entirely too much pride for their own good. They are too proud to beg, and would rather give than receive.

Since these people are so very wretched and unhappy when undeveloped and capable of such great success and happiness when awakened, they should need no urging to turn away from the lower tendencies and seek the enlightenment of truth and right living. No harmony is possible to them until they have learned self-control, but when that is attained they can become among the happiest and most successful people on earth.

The Cusp — Gemini and Cancer.

(June 21 to 27.)

The pursuit of pleasure seems to those born at this period, the only thing worth while in life.

This tendency is manifested at an early age, and every possible care should be taken that the children of this cusp may be guarded aright and their footsteps guided by a vigilant eye and a firm and loving hand. They are inclined to be reckless and wayward, and will neglect all other matters to seek amusement and pleasure.

The people of this cusp are fond of dress, and their great magnetic qualities make them very attractive. They are the most plausible of talkers, and are able to persuade or induce others to courses of action even against the better judgment of the ones influenced.

Particularly in money matters is this persuasive power in evidence. The men have no difficulty in obtaining control of the purse strings of their women friends, while the women, with their ingratiating manners, and wheedling tones, find it a simple matter to secure liberal "loans" without security.

Losses or gains mean very little to these people. If they meet with temporary failure in one direction, it seems to be only a stepping stone by aid of which they quickly regain their feet. "Backers" and "angels" — to use a theatrical term — are not long wanting for people of this cusp.

While brilliant in conversation and able to produce convincing arguments, it is frequently found that they are quite superficial, without great depth of feeling, knowledge or character.

In their constant search for pleasurable emotions and sensations they do not hesitate to sacrifice every other consideration. Broken promises, neglected engagements, inattention to business, even the loss of honor itself cannot deter them from seeking the gratification of this inordinate love of entertainment and pleasure.

Marital vows set lightly upon many of the people, especially if such vows interfere with their selfish pursuit of mis-called happiness, and they are often untruthful and unscrupulous.

The women are very much attached to their young, and in case of divorce they will abandon all else and make any sacrifice to enable them to retain their children.

The Cusp — Cancer and Leo.

(July 22 to 28.)

People of this sign are witty, daring, ambitious, and sometimes unscrupulous.

They reach and hold the highest places among their fellow-men, by reason of their activity, intellect and sympathetic loyalty.

This is the period that frequently produces the most corrupt of our politicians that attain eminence. They are masters of the art of appealing to the various vulnerable points of their associates, and their brilliant minds — often amounting to positive genius — with their vaulting and daring ambition, give them the power of securing for themselves the preferment and advancement on which they have set their desires, even though better men may of necessity be sacrificed to their progress.

Their natures are intensely sympathetic, especially to those in distress, and they contribute freely and lavishly to their relief.

Loyalty to their friends is another of their traits, and no trouble or disgrace is sufficient to cause them to forsake those whom they have given their friendship.

These people are eager in the pursuit of fresh sensations and new pleasures, as well as positions of greater honor or opportunity.

When living on the higher plane they can readily reach the topmost heights in any direction, and with their hearty, enthusiastic, sympathetic natures they may easily become first among the best-loved and most honored of earth.

The Cusp — Leo and Virgo.

(August 22 to 28.)

The people of this sign are usually very intelligent, and have uncommonly persuasive and convincing manner.

They are not altogether happy or content with any but the very best and finest furnishings for their homes, and this love of nice things extends to their wearing apparel. They are fond of elaborate display in dressing, and at times are likely to carry this fondness to an undesirable extreme.

And they are quick to grow tired of their home surroundings and of their wearing apparel, and are constantly endeavoring to procure new and better and more elaborate trappings. Their financial circum-

8*

stances set the only limit to their proceedings in this respect.

These people are fond of outdoor exercises and pleasures, and find considerable enjoyment in the case of lawns, gardens, etc. They particularly appreciate outdoor life when conditions and circumstances will permit the wearing of loose fitting and graceful garments.

The women of this sign are very easily convinced by arguments set forth in a plausible, persuasive way.

This period has produced some very highly successful physicians and teachers.

The Cusp — Virgo and Libra.

(September 23 to 29.)

Those of this sign who are living the higher life are among the most lovable people in the world. They are very fascinating in personality, and are utterly unselfish and filled with the greatest kindness of manner and speech.

The arts and sciences are of the greatest interest to these people, and they acquire much proficiency in such pursuits when they devote their energies in those directions.

Love of the beautiful in all things is very highly developed in these people. In their homes, their dress, their gardens, they strive to secure harmonious and pleasing effects, and their true artistic sense enables them to achieve the happiest results.

This artistic talent is also manifested in many other ways. Some very famous and successful designers of ladies' wearing apparel have come from this period, as well as capable and competent artists in other lines.

The beauties of nature are a source of deep and abiding delight to those of this sign, and they greatly admire peaceful scenery of river lands, and the majestic views of lake and ocean.

Their happy dispositions win for them many warm friends, and their success and advancement in life is likely to be all that could be desired, so long as they cultivate their spiritual natures and live the true life of harmony and self-control.

The Cusp — Libra and Scorpio.

(October 23 to 29.)

This cannot be considered a very favorable sign, yet its advantages may be overcome by the exercise of determination and by striving to develop the stronger, better side of the nature, and the people of the sign will be richly repaid for their perseverance.

These people are naturally creative geniuses, and are capable of extraordinary originality.

They also have much executive ability and are competent to carry to a successful termination any projects to which they apply themselves.

People born at this period are, as a rule, exceedingly tenacious of whatever positions they may have obtained, and will manage to retain their places in the face of almost any opposition or discouragement.

They are not always bothered with any particular scruples, nor do they appear to hold the truth in the consideration it deserves.

Some unrevealed power seems to enable them to get out of difficulties with great facility, and they emerge from the most complicated or hazardous predicaments with the utmost ease and confident assurance.

They are usually well liked by their companions, and are of pleasing personality. At the same time they have considerable jealousy in their composition, and this causes them more unhappiness than they are willing to admit.

It has been the writer's observation that where the influence of Libra is exerted just previous to a crisis in the life of a Libra-Scorpio person, as for instance a momentous business deal, a surgical operation, or a change of residence, at such times there is in evidence great anxiety, unreasoning fear, and lack of confidence.

It is just at such times as these that the Libra-Scorpio person has the greatest need of self-confidence and determination; and when these are cultivated and exercised, the result will be complete success.

The women of this sign are almost as good executives as the men. They are superior cooks, and display great tact and skill in the management of their households.

The Cusp — Scorpio and Sagittarius.

(November 22 to 28.)

Courage and determination seem to be the most marked characteristics of people born at this period, and their courage is of the active variety and their determination such that it carries them undaunted through many crises.

They have the faculty of acquiring knowledge not only from books but from observation and by absorption. The knowledge so acquired they can turn to practical account too, being especially clever at reproducing, duplicating or closely imitating anything they may have the opportunity to examine or observe.

In situations or circumstances where fearlessness, energy and an invincible determination are needed or desirable, these people are well adapted to meet all requirements with complete success.

They sometimes take upon themselves burdens and responsibility that seem beyond their strength, but their clear grit and enormous reserve power of strength enable them to carry these loads, and endure the stress, where weaker natures would fail utterly.

This period has produced some very famous surgeons — a vocation that demands supreme coolness, self-confidence and courage.

These people are either exceedingly disagreeable or exceedingly pleasant, — there seems to be no middle course possible to them. When cultured, they are the most fascinating and companionable persons one would care to meet.

With the women of this sign, the will power and courage is evidenced by their admirable power of discipline over their servants and their household organizations.

Their love of approbation is very marked, and unless this approbation is given them fully and frequently, they make themselves quite unhappy.

They should endeavor to banish all tendency to worry and fret, and to learn that these things are absolutely useless, accomplishing no good whatever.

Many remarkable talents are the natural heritage of these people, and those who learn and practice patience and passivity, as they fearlessly go on their appointed way, can reach the very greatest heights.

The Cusp — Sagittarius and Capricorn.

(December 21 to 27.)

Those who come into the world at this time are of Jovial and happy dispositions, fond of the good things of life, and demanding its best gifts for themselves and for those they love.

They have keen intellectual powers and are close observers. Some of the greatest minds, the deepest thinkers in the world have come out of the sign of this cusp. Excellent critics and writers, and some of the most eminent kindergarten teachers, are also numbered among its products.

Method in all things is a very strong attribute of these people, and this characteristic helps them on to the great successes they achieve in carrying out stupendous undertakings.

They are inclined to be exacting in their demands of others, but in compensation they are broad minded and liberal in dealing with their fellows.

They are not reckless nor incautious, but when they set their hands and minds to any undertaking they are in it to win — and win they invariably do, having great capacity for accomplishing their objects.

These people are apt and ready in conversation, and can acquit themselves most creditably in any company. The "gift of tongues" is theirs, and they make excellent linguists, acquiring fluency in and command of several languages with great facility.

To those of this sign who have any musical talent whatever, the author wishes to give his most earnest advice to cultivate this talent, by all means. The possibilities of high attainment in this line are very promising, and the time and energy devoted to musical culture and education will be paid for a thousand fold.

These people are extremely fond of children, and display remarkable patience and adaptability in their case.

They are also fond of the dance, becoming masters of the art and making excellent instructors therein.

The Cusp — Capricorn and Aquarius.

(January 20 to 26.)

This is a very favorable cusp, denoting great originality and versatility.

Persons born in this sign are not restricted in their choice of occupation or profession. They can usually succeed at anything they take up, and they are so versatile that they can sometimes pursue a half-dozen different lines and make money in all of them. They are the "jacks of all trades," but it cannot be said that they are "masters of none."

This is true of the women as well as of the men, and the author of this work has frequently been impressed with the fact that a large number of our most successful women in finance, commerce and manufacturing have been born under this personal magnet.

The men of this sign are exceedingly self-possessed and cool in their transactions, and are very strict, methodical, exacting, and sometimes very obstinate.

One potent reason for this general success is found

in their practice of economy, which is almost a religion to them. Nevertheless, they are very generous in many ways, but prefer to be their own judges as to what causes they shall contribute to.

They are often found in philanthropic work, and find much pleasure therein. Yet they are likely to withdraw from such interests without a moment's notice, especially where their philanthropy entails any neglect of other duties.

They display a high degree of pride in their social and intellectual achievements.

To entertain others is a strong desire of these people, and they succeed well in this, being brilliant speakers, and capable of adopting many original sayings that greatly impress their hearers.

These people should strictly observe the injunctions concerning marriage as set forth under the signs of Capricorn or Aquarius. This is of the gravest importance, as people of this Cusp are frequently bitterly disappointed in their social affairs.

The Cusp — Aquarius and Pisces.

(February 19 to 25.)

Persons born in this cusp are most frequently upright in character and just and honorable in all their dealings.

They have considerable desire to accumulate sufficient wealth to make them independent; and this leads them to be prompt and punctual in their business engagements. They live up to every promise or obligation to their customers and clients.

In social matters, however, where there is no money to be made or lost, they are not so careful, nor do they consider social engagements, apparently of sufficient importance as to be held inviolate. If reproached with having broken a social appointment they content themselves by expressing the opinion that their presence or absence would have made little difference, and therefore was not a matter of any moment.

They are warm hearted and generous people, always glad when they can be of assistance to others who may be less favored than themselves.

Ordinarily, they are among the best dressed people one encounters, but at times their taste in colors goes beyond the limits of good taste, even to displeasing extremes.

They do not lack of self appreciation, and frequently appear to find great delight in extolling their own virtues or telling of their accomplishments.

Marriage is a very serious matter to persons born at this period, and they should exercise the greatest care and deliberation in choosing their mates, for their marriages, if happy, are as much so as marriages can be, but if unhappy they are miserable and wretched to the last degree.

The Cusp — Pisces and Aries.

(March 21 to 27.)

The composition of this cusp is a most favorable and desirable one, indicating a union of the head — intelligence — and the feet — understanding. In effect, it denotes that persons born at this period are likely to possess strong mental powers, and to be blessed with the priceless gift of understanding or comprehension.

These people are strikingly, just and honorable in all their relations with their fellow men, and are indeed fully worthy of the great trust and confidence they inspire in others.

Their powers of intuition are truly remarkable, and they very rarely go amiss when they rely upon their own judgment as formulated by their intuition.

They have extremely keen and valuable foresight in all matters of a financial nature, and can mentally work out in advance, the most brilliant schemes and projects, which they then proceed to execute with complete success.

Being naturally inclined toward financial affairs, and possessing the qualities that make for success in any calling, it is not surprising that these people should be able to achieve distinction and wealth in that field.

The people of this sign are very loyal to their friends, extremely kind in disposition, enthusiastic on every subject that interests them, and altogether very fascinating persons. Their minds are always busily engaged in devising plans for new enterprises and projects, and the novelty of a scheme is to them perhaps its chief attraction.

The men of this cusp are inclined to marry early in life, while the women, on the other hand, seem as greatly inclined toward single-blessedness, preferring to profit by the experience of others in matrimonial affairs.

Both men and women of this sign are naturally clean-minded and of admirable moral characters. There are few other signs or cusps that promise more felicity than this, if, those born therein will realize and take advantage of its favorable influences.

SEXOLOGY.

A few moments should be set aside each day, a time for deep meditation and self-analysis upon the more important meanings of life. A time when you should be alone in silence and seclusion, then allow the mind and body to relax its tensions and carefully reflect every fault that retard your progress, — come out into the glare of the light, yes come face to face with your conscience and go over repeatedly, and most carefully too, the great truths taught by astrology.

Planetary influences ever surround us and when you once have a glimpse into the higher planes or meanings of life, you will then know how shallow, narrow, and insignificant a human life may become, all for the lack of knowledge on this most important of subjects and to drag out an existence based upon appetites and fleeting passion, ignorance is the cause of all the strife, misery, and disease as well as the cause of the greater part of the poverty in the world to-day.

Make your higher nature — the intellect — rule the body by not permitting the lower or animal nature to have full sway, by so doing you can rise to a most lofty height and success will crown your efforts, surely the lust of sex and appetites are not the objects of our lives — if this was to be so, how shallow is the human mind — "ah nay," these gratifications must come to an end and how soon too, leaving a trail of human debris indelibly marked by base and secret habits — see those pimples on the forehead, — the pinholes or pits around the nose, — and the bumps upon the neck of those you pass in the streets — why all this? Surely there is a cause and in the elimination of this cause we shall find the cure. What is the most frequent cause of lumbago or pain in the back? The answer is most likely an uncontrolled sex nature. There are four out of the twelve zodiacal signs whose sex nature is unusually strong — of course not all in these signs, for some have risen above the mere gratification of their feelings — this does not mean that you shall eliminate your sex nature entirely, but to put it under the proper control of your judgment.

One cannot hope to succeed in any line of business or to rise to prominence in any profession until they have lifted their thoughts above mere animal indulgence, you can neither plan methodically, or think clearly, and failure awaits you in the end.

In animal life there is but two objects, the desire for food and the gratification of their feelings. But man, the highest of all creation was gifted with intelligence to control all the parts of his body, just here there is room for broad thought on a subject that is worthy of much consideration, we see the young maiden before marriage in all the blushes of youth, her eyes sparkle, her cheeks aglow, the step elastic, but later, a short time after marriage takes place, we see her again, a wonderful change has taken place in a few short months. Surely this can't be the design of nature, but in reality is the ignorance of the laws of nature You can scarcely associate her now with the bright memories of the one you used to know, her cheeks are pale, her eyes dim with heavy lines, the step no longer has the spring of youth. What about the young man? Why does he lean against the office desk? Why does he not stand erect? And why is he gapping so? And what makes his task a drudgery? What about the marks that are stamped upon his countenance? Each habit has left its traces marked upon the face. And so too, with the man who has stooped to crime. Who cannot read in the face of the criminal, the reflection of his life's habits? Who cannot read in the face and eyes, the heart of an honest man. One can never fall so low but what he can rise again; the rise depends entirely upon yourself, and again I may say, renew the attack and surely with perseverance you can accomplish your desires. Astrology only lights the way, you must rise as you have fallen, that is just. You can rise to a power among men and achieve the greatest success and honor in the world, but only, by lifting your thoughts above slavish animal indulgence.

Everyone should read the instructive pages 19, 20 and 21 on Special Horoscopes.

The Author, after numerous requests, has now under preparation a most valuable book covering *two* of the *world's greatest monsters,*

APPETITE AND PASSION,

a work that will go to show that the LUST OF SEX and the craving of *Alcoholic* Stimulants are destroying the nation with alarming rapidity. Many plain facts will be revealed on the Sex Principles that heretofore have been cloaked in scientific terms for the learned and the medical profession. Much knowledge will be given that every man and woman should know. This book will be off the press about January 1, 1912.

Price 25 cents per Copy.

Place your order at any time.

Address the Author and Publisher,

ALFRED F. SEWARD,
Author and Publisher,
1566 Bryden Road,
Columbus, Ohio.

NOTED PERSONAGES

Born in The Twelve Signs of the Zodiac.

ARIES.

(March 21 to April 19.)

General Ballington Booth (Salvationist)..April 10, 1829
Lawrence Barrett (actor)................April 4, 1838
Henry Clay, (statesman)..............April 12, 1777
Dr. S. B. Hartman.....................April 1, 1830
James Harper, (publisher) ....April 13, 1795
Chas. M. Schwab, (capitalist).........April 18, 1862

LEO.

(July 22 to August 22.)

David H. Agnew, (surgeon)..........August 8, 1830
Daniel Frohman, (theatrical manager).August 22, 1851
Henry Clews (financier)............August 14, 1840
Mary Anderson Navarro, (actress).....,July 28, 1859
Robert G. Dun, (R. G. Dun's Com. Agency)
                                     August 7, 1826
Wm. L. Douglas, (famous shoe mfg.).August 22, 1845
William Gillett, (actor and author).....July 24, 1853
Julia Marlowe, (actress)..............August 7, 1870
Chas. Pond, (Pond's extract)........August 20, 1820

SAGITTARIUS.

(November 22 to December 21.)

August Belmont, (banker).........December 8, 1816
Daniel Appleton, (publisher).......December 10, 1785
John Greenleaf Whittier, (poet)....December 17, 1807
Richard Croker, "Boss of N. Y.."...November 24, 1843
John H. Patterson, National Cash Register
    Co. ....December 13, 1844
Samuel L. Clemens, "Mark Twain"..November 30, 1835
H. C. Frick, (Coke and steel mfg.)..December 19, 1849

GEMINI.

(May 20 to June 21.)

Miss Helen Gould, (philanthropist)......June 20, 1868
Richard Mansfield, (actor)..............May 24, 1857
William Aspinwall, (surgeon)...........May 23, 1743

LIBRA.

(September 23 to October 23.)

Denman Thompson, (actor and author, Old
   Homestead) ....…....October 15, 1853
H. J. Heinz, (pickle king)...........October 11, 1844
Geo. Westinghouse, (elec. appliances).October 18, 1864
Jenny Lind, (opera singer)............October 6, 1821
Edward W. Bok, (editor Ladies' Home Jour-
   nal) ....…......October 9, 1863
Thomas Nast, (editor Harper's Weekly)
                        September 18, 1840

AQUARIUS.

(January 20 to February 19.)

Henry Watterson, (editor Louisville Courier-
   Journal) ....February 16, 1844
Wm. Colgate, (soap mfg.)...........…...January 25, 1853
Francis Wilson, (actor)............February 4, 1854
Robert Mantell, (actor)….............February 7, 1854
Peter Cooper, (founder Cooper Institute, N.
   Y.) ....…....February 12, 1791
Cyrus H. McCormick, (inventor harvesting
   machinery) ....February 21, 1834
Thomas A. Edison, (inventor)......February 11, 1847
Wm. McKinley ....…...January 29, 1843

TAURUS.

(April 19 to May 20.)

Geo. W. Childs, (philanthropist)........May 12, 1829
O. Mergenthaler, (inventor type-setting machinery) ....……..**May 11, 1845**

Phil Armour, (packer).................May 16, 1832
General U. S. Grant...................April 27, 1822
Wm. T. Bull, (surgeon)................May 18, 1849
Moritz Rosenthal, (attorney)...........May 4, 1866
Ada Rehan, (actress)..................April 22, 1860
C. H. Cramp, (ship builder)...........May 9, 1829

VIRGO.
(August 22 to September 23.)

R. M. Hoe, (inv. printing press)...September 12, 1812
James J. Hill, (R. R. financier)....September 12, 1838
Daniel H. Buchanan, (architect)....September 4, 1864
Robert C. Clowery, (Pres. W. U. Tel. Co.)..
September 8, 1838
Charles Dana Gibson, (artist)......September 14, 1867

CAPRICORN.
(December 21 to January 20.)

Henry Steinway, (piano mfg.)........January 3, 1857
Horatio Alger, Jr., (author).........January 13, 1832
Henry M. Flagler, (capitalist).......January 2, 1830
Frederick B. Opper, (comic artist)....January 2, 1857
Clay Clements, (actor)...........December 21, 1863
Joseph A. Jeffrey, (Jeffrey Mfg. Co)..January 17, 1836
Chas. Goodyear, (rubber mfg.).....December 29, 1800

CANCER.
(June 21 to July 22.)

P. T. Barnum, (showman)...............July 5, 1810
Elias Howe, (inv. sewing mach.)........July 9, 1819
Geo. Eastman, (inv. of the Kodak)......June 12, 1854
Henry Ward Beecher, (clergyman)......June 24, 1813
Augustin Daly, (actor and theatrical mgr.)
July 20, 1838
Chauncy Alcott, (actor)................July 21, 1859
Joseph B. Foraker......................July 5, 1846
John Wanamaker.......................July 11, 1837

SCORPIO.

(October 23 to November 22.)

John Philip Sousa.................November 6, 1854
Maud Adams, (actress)...........November 11, 1872
John Drew, (actor)..............November 13, 1845
Geo. A. Macbeth, (lamp chimney mfg.).....
                              October 29, 1845
Joseph W. Folk....................October 28, 1869
Eugene V. Debs...................November 5, 1855
L. E. Waterman, (fountain pens)..November 20, 1837

PISCES.

(February 19 to March 21.)

Augustus Saint Gaudens, (sculptor)....March 1, 1848
Washington L. Atlee, (surgeon)....February 22, 1808
Luther Burbank ....March 7, 1849
Stuart Robson, (actor)................March 4, 1836
Grover Cleveland ....March 13, 1837
Abraham Lincoln ....February 12, 1809
George Washington ....February 22, 1732

COSIMO is a specialty publisher of books and publications that inspire, inform and engage readers. Our mission is to offer unique books to niche audiences around the world.

COSIMO CLASSICS offers a collection of distinctive titles by the great authors and thinkers throughout the ages. At COSIMO CLASSICS timeless classics find a new life as affordable books, covering a variety of subjects including: *Biographies, Business, History, Mythology, Personal Development, Philosophy, Religion and Spirituality,* and much more!

COSIMO-on-DEMAND publishes books and publications for innovative authors, non-profit organizations and businesses. COSIMO-on-DEMAND specializes in bringing books back into print, publishing new books quickly and effectively, and making these publications available to readers around the world.

COSIMO REPORTS publishes public reports that affect your world: from global trends to the economy, and from health to geo-politics.

FOR MORE INFORMATION CONTACT US AT
INFO@COSIMOBOOKS.COM

❋ If you are a book-lover interested in our current catalog of books.

❋ If you are an author who wants to get published

❋ If you represent an organization or business seeking to reach your members, donors or customers with your own books and publications

**COSIMO BOOKS ARE ALWAYS
AVAILABLE AT ONLINE BOOKSTORES**

VISIT COSIMOBOOKS.COM
BE INSPIRED, BE INFORMED